THE ULTIMATE STEP-BY-STEP DEMENTIA CAREGIVER'S GUIDE

Proven Methods to Improve Communication, Enhance Daily Life, Avoid Stress and Burnout, and Navigate the Healthcare System

SHEA WOLFE

Disclaimer

This guide is intended to provide information and support for individuals caring for loved ones with dementia. It is not intended to serve as a substitute for professional medical advice, diagnosis, or treatment. Readers are encouraged to consult with qualified healthcare professionals regarding specific caregiving situations, medical conditions, treatments, and any questions or concerns they may have. The author disclaims liability for any loss or damage resulting from the guide's use. By using this guide, readers acknowledge and agree to the terms of this disclaimer.

CONTENTS

"The Lord is near to all who call on Him, to all who call on Him in truth."

— *PSALM* 145:18

INTRODUCTION

Every journey begins with a single step, yet when that path is caregiving for someone with dementia, those steps can feel uncertain, overwhelming, and profoundly isolating. The inspiration for this book came about during our personal experiences as caregivers, as my husband and I found ourselves engulfed by both practical and emotional challenges. My name is Shea Wolfe, and if there is one thing I have learned, it is that the journey of a dementia caregiver is as much about exploring the heart as it is about navigating the healthcare system. This book is my heartfelt response to that realization—a comprehensive guide designed to empower you with practical caregiving advice and address the emotional and psychological well-being of both the caregiver and the loved one.

Balancing empathetic support with evidence-based strategies serves as both a guide to caregiving tasks and a companion through the emotional journey of caring for someone with dementia. It draws support from real-life examples, tips, and advice rooted in the latest research and best practices in dementia care.

As you journey through these pages, let them remind you that you are not alone. Armed with knowledge and resources, you can navigate the caregiving journey with confidence, compassion, and a renewed sense of purpose. Here's to nurturing wellness with unwavering care, treasuring memories, and experiencing personal growth beyond imagination. Together, we will navigate this path with insights and strategies, confronting challenges with resilience and optimism.

CHAPTER 1

UNDERSTANDING DEMENTIA

Within the tapestry of medical terminology and caregiving narratives, dementia often emerges as a complex character, misunderstood by many and familiar to an unfortunate few. The gravity of its presence in the lives of those it touches—individuals diagnosed and their caregivers—cannot be emphasized enough. Yet, for all its prevalence and impact, dementia remains shrouded in misconception and mystery. This chapter aims to demystify dementia, separating fact from fiction and laying a foundation for understanding and effective caregiving.

WHAT IS DEMENTIA?

At its core, dementia represents a syndrome—a collection of symptoms rather than a singular disease. Understanding this difference is vital for grasping how extensive and significant it is. It manifests through a decline in cognitive functions such as memory, language, problem-solving, and other abilities critical to daily life. These are not mere lapses akin to forgetting where one left their keys. They are profound impairments that disrupt routine tasks and can ultimately take away a person's independence.

Contrary to common belief, dementia's divergence from normal aging is stark. While aging may bring about mild changes in memory, dementia delineates itself with significant, life-altering deterioration. The distinction lies in how drastic cognitive abilities decline, moving beyond the expected wear and tear of years to a realm where support and intervention become necessities.

Delving into the cerebral underpinnings of dementia unveils a landscape where the brain itself undergoes profound changes. Regions responsible for memory, reasoning, and emotion control, among others, are severely affected, leading to the symptoms observed. It is an insidious process, often creeping in silently before its effects become unmistakably clear. The brain, a complex organ, finds itself compromised, its usual pathways obstructed and altered, giving rise to the challenges characteristic of dementia.

Recognizing these symptoms early stands as a beacon for those navigating the uncertain waters of dementia care. Prompt recognition not only offers a chance for individuals and families to plan and manage care effectively but also opens avenues for interventions. This underlines the importance of vigilance and awareness, traits that caregivers and loved ones must cultivate to find their way through the evolving terrain of dementia care.

Visual Elements: Interactive Checklist for Early Recognition of Dementia Symptoms

To aid in the early recognition of dementia, consider the following interactive checklist. It encompasses common signs that may indicate the need for a professional evaluation:

- Recent Memory Loss Affecting Daily Activities: Forgetting recently learned information, important dates, or events; repeatedly asking for the same information.
- Difficulty Performing Familiar Tasks: Challenges in planning or solving problems; trouble completing familiar tasks at home, work, or leisure.
- Problems with Language: Struggling to follow or join a conversation; trouble finding the right word or calling things by the wrong name.
- Disorientation to Time and Place: Losing track of current location, dates, seasons, and passage of time; needing help understanding something if it is not happening immediately.
- Poor or Decreased Judgment: Experiencing changes in judgment or decision-making, such as paying less attention to grooming or keeping clean, losing awareness of consequences and risk.
- Problems with Abstract Thinking: Difficulty dealing with numbers and using abstract concepts.
- Misplacing Items: Placing things in unusual places; inability to retrace their steps to find lost items.
- Changes in Mood or Behavior: Mood swings for no apparent reason, such as becoming confused, suspicious, depressed, fearful, or anxious.

- Changes in Personality: Becoming irritable, easily upset, or even aggressively angry out of character.

This checklist is not exhaustive but serves as a starting point. If multiple items on this list raise concerns, it is advisable to consult a healthcare professional for a comprehensive evaluation.

In understanding dementia, one confronts a medical condition and a call to empathy and swift action. The decline in cognitive abilities that defines this condition challenges us to rethink our approach to care, communication, and support. It demands a blend of knowledge, patience, and creativity to ensure that those living with dementia can do so with dignity and as much independence as possible. As we progress through this exploration, keep in mind the human element at the heart of it all —the individuals and families navigating this condition daily. Their experiences, struggles, and triumphs can help pave the road forward, guiding us toward a deeper understanding and more effective caregiving approaches.

UNDERSTANDING THE DIFFERENT TYPES OF DEMENTIA

Diving into the complexities of dementia reveals a panorama marked by diversity. Various forms of the condition manifest through unique patterns of cognitive decline. This section unravels the intricacies of the most prevalent types of dementia, shedding light on their distinct characteristics and underlying causes.

Alzheimer's Disease

Alzheimer's disease, the most common type of dementia, slowly affects cognitive abilities by causing memory loss and difficulty with reasoning. It starts with forgetting recent events or conversations and worsens over time, affecting broader memory and thinking abilities. As the disease progresses, daily tasks become harder, and language, spatial awareness, and personality changes become noticeable. Alzheimer's disease follows a variable pace but eventually requires comprehensive care.

Vascular Dementia

Vascular dementia disrupts cognitive function by affecting the brain's blood supply, often caused by strokes or conditions that block blood flow. Symptoms can appear suddenly after a stroke or gradually over time, affecting memory, planning, and reasoning abilities. Managing blood pressure and cholesterol can help reduce the risk. This type of dementia highlights the link between cardiovascular health and cognitive well-being, stressing the importance of lifestyle choices in prevention.

Lewy Body Dementia

Lewy body dementia is characterized by microscopic protein deposits called Lewy bodies, which cause a mix of cognitive, physical, and psychiatric symptoms. Memory loss combined with muscle stiffness, tremors, and visual problems, including hallucinations, creates a complex clinical picture. You might have healthy eyes but have some visual difficulties. These problems are caused by the effects of dementia on the brain. Sleep problems, including acting out dreams during REM sleep, add to the complexity. Given the presence of Lewy bodies in the brain and its varied symptoms, clinicians need to conduct individual research to understand its neurodegenerative processes better.

Frontotemporal Dementia

Frontotemporal dementia affects behavior, personality, and language due to changes in the brain's frontal and temporal lobes. Unlike other dementias with prominent memory loss, frontotemporal dementia often starts with subtle social or language changes. Damage to these brain regions alters social cues and language skills, affecting a person's identity and communication abilities. This type of dementia challenges our understanding of personality and identity rooted in the brain's neural networks.

Dementia comes in various forms, each with unique origins and symptoms, highlighting the need for personalized care. Whether it is the gradual decline of Alzheimer's, sudden changes after a stroke in Vascular dementia, the varied symptoms of Lewy Body dementia, or behavioral and language changes in Frontotemporal dementia, the impact on individuals and families is significant. This diversity requires tailored clinical approaches and collective responses to dementia that consider each person's unique needs and experiences.

RECOGNIZING THE EARLY SIGNS AND SYMPTOMS

In dementia, signs often start quietly before becoming obvious, blending into daily life. These early indicators of cognitive decline may seem like normal forgetfulness due to aging but when combined, suggest early-stage dementia. This phase offers a chance for intervention to slow progression and preserve quality of life.

Memory Loss that Disrupts Daily Life

One of the earliest signs of dementia is memory loss, which begins to disrupt routine living. It is more than just temporarily forgetting names or locations of objects; it is a consistent struggle to remember recent events, conversations, appointments, and even personal care. This creates a gap in one's daily life, where moments slip away quickly. Family members often notice this symptom and recognize it as a sign that further evaluation is needed.

Challenges in Planning or Solving Problems

Another early sign of dementia is the loss of the ability to plan or solve problems, which are essential for independent living. Simple tasks like balancing a checkbook or following recipes become difficult and confusing. This decline in executive functions highlights the challenges of dementia, making life more complicated for those affected and indicating deeper cognitive issues.

Confusion with Time or Place

In the early stages of dementia, individuals often experience disorientation, making it difficult to know the time or place. It is more than occasional forgetfulness about the day; it is like being in a constant fog where time and space seem unclear. Seasons blend together, and time becomes distorted, leaving individuals feeling lost in their own lives. Even familiar places can feel strange, turning homes into confusing mazes and streets into unknown areas. This confusion not only makes it hard to navigate but also increases the risk of accidents, emphasizing the need for early detection and support.

Trouble Understanding Visual Images and Spatial Relationships

In dementia, trouble understanding visual images and spatial relationships can surprise families. It is more than just vision problems; it affects how individuals see and interact with the world. Reading becomes harder as words blur, and judging distances becomes challenging, making tasks like driving or moving around the house more difficult. Colors and contrasts may seem dull, reducing visual enjoyment. While not as recognized as memory loss, these difficulties greatly impact daily life, making self-care and safety more challenging. They signal the need for thorough evaluation and support.

Recognizing early signs of dementia involves noticing various symptoms that disrupt one's life. From memory loss to problems with planning and spatial awareness, these signs call for attention and action. Addressing them promptly offers a chance to slow down the advancement of the condition and maintain independence. It is important to seek guidance and support to navigate this avenue effectively.

THE DIFFERENT STAGES

The Early Stage

In the early stages of dementia, subtle changes begin to appear, often unnoticed by most people. While symptoms are mild, they hint at deeper changes. People may struggle with forgetfulness beyond typical memory lapses, but yet can still manage daily tasks independently. They may start using notes or digital reminders to help them remember things. Social activities and hobbies may still interest them, though they might participate less intensely. This phase involves adapting to these changes while trying to maintain a sense of normalcy. Caregivers, new to their role, may notice these changes with concern and disbelief, grappling with the idea of a diagnosis that still feels distant.

The Middle Stage

As dementia progresses to the middle stage, noticeable changes occur. What used to be subtle becomes more obvious as the person's ability to function independently declines. Memory problems deepen, making it hard to recognize faces and recall memories. Daily tasks become harder and require more help. Language skills start to decline, causing frustration in communication. It is a difficult stage where the person's essence seems to fade away due to dementia symptoms. Caregivers take on more responsibilities, helping with personal care, medications, and safety, all while dealing with the emotional strain of watching their loved one deteriorate.

The Late Stage

In the late stage of dementia, individuals become increasingly disconnected from the world around them. Communication may be reduced to non-verbal cues or absent altogether because they lose the capacity to recognize speech. They lose the ability to recognize time and place, engage with their environment, or enjoy simple pleasures. Physical abilities decline along with cognitive functions, often resulting in limited mobility, and the inability to eat, walk, and use the toilet without assistance. Round-the-clock care becomes necessary, whether at home or in a specialized facility. Caregiving shifts focus to providing comfort, dignity, and relief from discomfort. This stage is characterized by attentive care while bracing for loss.

CAREGIVING THROUGH THE STAGES

Caring for someone with dementia is like charting a course through unfamiliar territory, where every step is uncertain. In the early stage, caregivers provide support and make subtle adjustments to help maintain the person's independence while learning about the condition and preparing for what lies ahead.

As dementia progresses, caregiver responsibilities increase, requiring more direct involvement in daily tasks and decision-making. Communication becomes more challenging, and caregivers must adapt to new ways of connecting with their loved ones. The emotional toll grows as they mourn the person's gradual loss and cope with the demands of caregiving.

In the late stage, caregiving focuses on providing comfort and managing symptoms. This period is emotionally draining as caregivers confront the impending loss while striving to ensure the person's final days are peaceful. A strong support network, including family, healthcare professionals, and hospice care teams, becomes essential.

Navigating dementia requires flexibility, tenacity, and an ever-evolving approach to care. Caregivers face love, loss, and constant change as they adjust to the demands of each stage. It is a transformative role that demands continuous learning, adaptation, and strength to face each day with hope and determination.

NEUROLOGICAL CHANGES

Dementia is characterized by significant changes in the brain, which result from a variety of physical and chemical alterations.

Abnormal protein buildup, such as amyloid plaques and tau tangles, is commonly observed in the brains of individuals with dementia, particularly in conditions like Alzheimer's disease. These protein aggregates can disrupt brain cell function and eventually lead to cell death, contributing to the progressive decline in cognitive abilities.

Additionally, the impairment of neurotransmitter systems is often associated with dementia. Neurotransmitters are chemical messengers that facilitate communication between neurons in the brain. Disruptions in neurotransmitter function can hinder effective signaling between brain cells, further impacting cognitive function and leading to symptoms like memory loss, confusion, and impaired reasoning.

The causes of abnormal protein buildup in the brain, such as amyloid plaques and tau tangles, are complex and poorly understood. However, several factors are believed to contribute to their formation:

- Genetic factors: Some forms of dementia, particularly Alzheimer's disease, have genetic components that can increase the risk of abnormal protein accumulation. Mutations in specific genes, such as the amyloid precursor protein (APP) gene or genes related to tau protein production, can contribute to the development of amyloid plaques and tau tangles.
- Environmental factors: Environmental factors such as head trauma, exposure to certain toxins or chemicals, and chronic stress may play a role in the accumulation of abnormal proteins in the brain. These factors can contribute to the disruption of normal protein processing and clearance mechanisms.

- Abnormal protein processing and clearance: In individuals with dementia, there is evidence that the normal processes of protein folding, aggregation, and clearance are disrupted. This can lead to the accumulation of misfolded proteins, such as amyloid-beta and tau, which form plaques and tangles in the brain.
- Inflammatory processes: Chronic inflammation in the brain, which can result from various factors including infection, autoimmune diseases, or vascular problems, may contribute to the accumulation of abnormal proteins. Inflammation can disrupt normal cellular functions and exacerbate the production and aggregation of amyloid-beta and tau proteins.

Overall, the development of abnormal protein buildup in the brain is likely influenced by a combination of genetic, environmental, and age-related factors, as well as disruptions in protein processing and clearance mechanisms. Understanding these underlying mechanisms is crucial for developing effective treatments and interventions for dementia and related neurodegenerative diseases.

Brain Regions Affected

Dementia manifests through the impairment of distinct brain regions, each contributing to a range of symptoms.

- Hippocampus: Vital for memory and learning functions, is typically one of the earliest areas affected, leading to memory deficits.
- Frontal Lobe: This governs reasoning and emotional regulation and can result in impaired judgment, perception of consequence, and personality alterations.

- Parietal Lobes: These are responsible for processing sensory information and spatial awareness. They contribute to language impairments and difficulties in recognizing objects and faces.

Targeting specific brain regions explains the many symptoms of dementia, making it very complex and challenging.

COGNITIVE VS. NON-COGNITIVE SYMPTOMS

Cognitive symptoms of dementia are related to thinking and processing information. They include problems like memory loss, difficulty with language, and trouble solving problems. These symptoms happen because the brain is deteriorating. They make it harder for people to do things like remember names or follow instructions.

Non-cognitive symptoms, on the other hand, affect emotions and behaviors. They include mood swings and aggression. These symptoms also come from changes in the brain, but they show up as changes in how people feel and act. This means that dementia affects not only thinking but also emotions and behavior.

Understanding the difference between these two types of symptoms helps us see how dementia impacts people differently. Caregivers and medical professionals must recognize both types of symptoms to manage the challenges of dementia effectively.

Dealing with Loss of Independence

Losing independence is one of the hardest parts of dementia. Tasks and decisions that used to be easy become overwhelming, making people rely on others for everyday things like dressing and eating. This loss of abilities and identity is deeply upsetting. It is important to create a supportive environment where the person's remaining abilities are encouraged, and their independence is respected as much as possible.

Fear and Confusion

People often become fearful and confused as their memory declines. Familiar places become strange, and memories become fragmented, leading to a deep sense of disorientation and anxiety. This fear is understandable as the world no longer follows the usual rules and logic. The confusion extends beyond forgetting names and faces to a fundamental loss of time and place, making everyday life bewildering. As a result, there's a fear of losing even more—memories, relationships, and one's sense of self. Providing empathetic care is crucial in offering reassurance and stability during this turbulent time.

Depression and Anxiety

Depression and anxiety are common in people with dementia, often blending with the disease itself. They can worsen the challenges, making people feel more isolated and lost. Depression brings sadness and disinterest, making it hard to engage with others. While anxiety makes fears seem worse, causing more distress, loss of trust, and even paranoid delusions. These emotions are not just side effects of cognitive decline; they show the deep struggle people face as they lose their abilities. Treating these conditions needs more than just medication; it requires a deeply caring approach that considers both the emotional and physical aspects of dementia care.

DISPELLING MYTHS

In the realm of health; myths and misunderstandings about this condition are widespread. One common belief is that dementia is simply a part of getting older, but this is not accurate. Dementia actually arises from various brain diseases and injuries, not just from aging. It is important to recognize this distinction to approach these diseases with empathy and to develop effective treatments.

Confusion can often arise when people compare normal memory lapses in aging with memory loss in dementia. While occasional forgetfulness is common, dementia causes significant memory impairment that affects daily life and personal identity. Recognizing this difference helps us understand the seriousness of this condition and the need for compassionate care.

Misconceptions about dementia being curable with current treatments can lead to false hope or unnecessary despair. While some treatments may offer temporary relief of symptoms or even slow the progression, there is currently no cure. Understanding this reality can significantly help manage expectations while emphasizing the importance of ongoing research.

Dementia is often associated with stigma and isolation due to fear and misunderstanding. This stigma can lead to social withdrawal, denial, and reluctance to seek help, worsening the challenges for individuals and families. Confronting this stigma is essential for a more supportive and inclusive social acceptance.

It's typical for individuals with dementia to resist acknowledging their condition, so engage them in conversations about any changes they've observed in themselves or specific challenges they're facing. This approach could prompt them to open up about their emotions, allowing you to offer reassurance or propose support options. Avoid directly challenging or persuading them about their diagnosis.

Addressing these myths and misconceptions requires factual accuracy and compassion. By dispelling these misunderstandings, we can develop a more informed and empathetic approach, recognizing the complexity of the condition and the dignity of those affected. This shift in understanding informs policies, practices, and personal interactions, improving the experience for individuals and families worldwide.

THE ROLE OF GENETICS

Genetics plays a subtle but complex role in determining risk. Inheriting certain genes from our parents can increase the likelihood of developing dementia, but it does not mean it's inevitable. These genetic factors interact with other internal and environmental factors, influencing the chances of acquiring this disorder.

Some forms of dementia, like familial Alzheimer's disease, show a direct pattern of inheritance due to mutations in specific genes like APP, PSEN1, and PSEN2. However, these cases are rare. In more common forms, such as sporadic Alzheimer's, many genes contribute to susceptibility in a less clear-cut way. The APOE gene, especially its E4 variant, is a well-known risk factor but does not guarantee dementia. It does, however, affect the odds. This genetic predisposition, lifestyle choices, environmental factors, and other health conditions create a complex and individualized risk profile for each individual.

Genetic Testing and Counseling

Gene testing offers both promise and caution in the realm of dementia genetics. While it can provide clarity about one's genetic risk for developing dementia, it also brings the factor of foresight. Through DNA analysis, genetic testing can identify mutations linked to hereditary dementia and reveal risk factors like the APOE-e4 allele. Those who inherit one copy of APOE-e4 from their mother or father have an increased risk of developing Alzheimer's. Those who inherit two copies from their mother and father have an even higher risk, but not a certainty. In addition to raising risk, APOE-e4 may tend to make symptoms appear at a younger age than usual. However, this knowledge must be handled with care and sensitivity.

Deciding whether to undergo genetic testing for dementia requires careful consideration. Genetic counseling is essential in navigating the emotional and practical implications of the results. Counselors, skilled in genetic study and communication, interpret test results and help individuals and families understand the level of risk, the limitations of current predictions, and the absence of definitive treatments for dementia. This supportive dialogue aims to empower rather than overwhelm, shedding light on genetic knowledge without dictating choices.

Risk Reduction Through Lifestyle

In the relationship between genes and dementia, reducing risk is a way to take control of our health. While our genetic makeup affects our chances of getting dementia, it does not mean we are doomed. Our genes interact with lifestyle factors we can change, like diet, exercise, mental activity, and social connections. By making healthy choices, we can lower our risk of dementia.

Maintaining a healthy diet is essential for overall well-being, including brain health and reducing the risk of dementia. Here are some dietary recommendations to consider:

- Mediterranean Diet: This diet emphasizes fruits, vegetables, whole grains, nuts, seeds, and healthy fats like olive oil. It also includes moderate amounts of fish, poultry, and dairy, with limited red meat intake. The Mediterranean diet has been associated with a reduced risk of dementia and overall cognitive decline.
- Eat Fatty Fish: Fish like Salmon, Mackerel, Tuna, and Sardines are rich in omega-3 fatty acids, which are beneficial for brain health. Aim to include fatty fish in your diet at least two to three times a week.
- Increase Antioxidant Intake: Antioxidants help protect the brain from oxidative stress, which can contribute to diminished mental functions. Include foods rich in antioxidants such as blueberries and strawberries, dark leafy greens, nuts, and seeds, and colorful vegetables like broccoli, bell peppers, tomatoes, and carrots.
- Limit Sugar and Refined Carbohydrates: Diets high in sugar and refined carbohydrates have been linked to an increased risk of cognitive decline. Limit your sugary snacks and desserts and opt for whole grains like oats, quinoa, and whole wheat bread instead.
- Minimal Alcohol Consumption: Excessive alcohol consumption can increase the risk of dementia. However, it is best not to drink at all.
- Stay Hydrated: Proper hydration is essential for brain function and overall health. Drink plenty of filtered water; black tea and herbal teas are great. Also, limit your

intake of sugary or caffeinated beverages like sodas and excessive coffee.

- Control Portion Sizes: Overeating can lead to obesity and other health problems that may increase the risk of dementia. Pay attention to portion sizes and avoid eating to the point of feeling overly full.

- Intermittent Fasting: May help regulate blood sugar levels, reduce inflammation, enhance brain function, and support cellular repair processes. However, individual responses to intermittent fasting can vary, and it may not be suitable for everyone, especially those with certain medical conditions or dietary needs.

- Eliminate Trans Fats: Diets high in trans fats have been associated with an increased risk of cognitive decline. Limit your intake of foods high in these fats, such as commercial baked goods such as cakes, cookies, and pies, shortening, microwave popcorn, frozen pizza, refrigerated dough such as biscuits and rolls, fried foods, including french fries, doughnuts, and fried chicken, nondairy coffee creamer, stick margarine, and processed foods.

- Consider Dietary Supplements: Consult with a healthcare professional before taking any dietary supplements, but some nutrients, such as omega 3, vitamin D, vitamin C, B vitamins, mushrooms, and ashwagandha, which is also good for relaxing, are beneficial for brain health when taken as part of a balanced diet.

- Stay Socially Active: While not directly related to diet, maintaining social connections and engaging in mentally stimulating activities can help preserve cognitive function as you age.

Remember, maintaining a healthy lifestyle involves more than just diet. Regular physical exercise, adequate sleep, stress management, and intellectual stimulation are also important factors in reducing the risk of dementia.

This combination of lifestyle choices, guided by our genetic risk, is not a surefire way to prevent dementia, but it is definitely taking a proactive approach. It recognizes genetics' influence while emphasizing everyday actions' impact on our health. By adopting a brain-healthy lifestyle, we're not just following advice—we're taking charge of our health, transcending genetic limitations.

COPING WITH A DEMENTIA DIAGNOSIS

Receiving a dementia diagnosis shakes up life as we know it, stirring a mix of emotions and decisions for individuals and their families. The news brings fear and uncertainty about what lies ahead, affecting everyone collectively but in different ways.

Obtaining accurate information and support is key during this tough time. Support groups and dementia organizations also provide insight and recommendations to others going through similar experiences.

As the shock wears off, planning for the future becomes crucial. Legal and financial matters, like wills and testaments, financial planning, and medical legalities, need intense attention to honor the person's wishes. Care plans, from daily support to long-term arrangements, aim to maintain the best quality of life possible throughout the dementia journey.

But amidst all the practical planning, there is a focus on living well, despite the conditions. Finding joy and fulfillment becomes important. Engaging in activities that bring happiness, making adjustments at home for safety and independence, and prioritizing nutrition and physical health all play a vital role in this.

Social connections also play a big part in maintaining well-being. Spending time with loved ones and participating in community activities can absolutely provide emotional support, stress reduction, and a well-needed sense of belonging.

Coping with a dementia diagnosis is not easy, but with support and planning, individuals and families can navigate the journey with courage and hope, finding moments of clarity and resilience along the way.

CHAPTER 2

CONNECTING THROUGH COMMUNICATION

Communication can be very challenging with dementia care, as cognitive decline affects understanding and expression. Adapting how we speak becomes crucial to bridging this gap. This chapter explores communication techniques for caregivers to help individuals with dementia feel understood and connected. It's important to remember they are likely to have sight or hearing problems as well, which can also make it harder for them to communicate.

People with dementia often experience changes in their emotional responses. They may have less control over their feelings and how to express them. For example, someone may overreact to things, have rapid mood changes, or feel irritable. They may also appear unusually distant or uninterested in things.

Individuals living with dementia may exhibit a range of challenging behaviors, including increased demands, restlessness, agitation, suspicion, disorientation, and hallucinations, particularly during nighttime hours. It is essential to respond to these behaviors with compassion and understanding. Providing reassurance and comfort can help alleviate distress and promote a sense of security for the individual.

Caregivers should prioritize creating a supportive and nurturing environment in times of heightened agitation or confusion. This may involve offering gentle reminders of familiar routines, engaging in calming activities such as listening to soothing music or providing a comforting touch, and validating the individual's feelings and experiences without judgment. Caregivers can foster a sense of emotional connection and well-being, ultimately enriching the quality of life for individuals living with dementia.

ADAPTING YOUR COMMUNICATION STYLE

Simplifying Language

When talking to someone with dementia, it's important to keep communication simple. Long, complicated sentences can be confusing to them. Stick to short, clear sentences that focus on one idea at a time. Think of it like finding your way through a forest: clear paths make the journey easier. Likewise, simple language helps them understand better and strengthens the bond between caregivers and persons with dementia. An example would be, "Let's try this way," instead of "Don't do this.", "Thanks for helping." even if the results aren't perfect.

Patience is Key

In dementia care, time does not move the same way it used to. Cognitive processes may slow down as individuals navigate through a maze of memories and thoughts, and responses may take longer as thoughts wander through memories. That is why patience is crucial. Giving the person ample time to process information and articulate their thoughts demonstrates a profound respect for their journey and their challenges.

Avoiding Open-Ended Questions

Too many choices can be overwhelming in dementia. It's like being lost in a maze. Simplifying questions can help. Instead of asking open-ended questions, offer simple choices or yes/no options. For example, "Are you tired?" instead of "How do you feel?", or "Do you want soup or salad?" instead of "What would you like to eat for lunch?" This makes decisions easier and less stressful. Try using different words if they don't understand the first time. Like if you ask them whether they are hungry and you don't get a response, you could say, "Dinner is ready now. Let's eat." Try not to say, "Don't you remember?" or "I told you."

Being Mindful of Tone and Volume

In communication, how we speak is just as important as what we say. The tone and volume of your voice can comfort or unsettle someone with dementia. Speaking gently and calmly can help ease fears, create a sense of security, look them in the eyes, and call them by their name. It's like guiding someone through calm waters instead of rough seas. Being mindful of how we speak shows our care and respect, even when dementia makes communication difficult.

Try this exercise to improve your communication:

Think about a recent conversation you had with your loved one. Find a message or question that could have been simpler. Rewrite it using simpler words and yes/no questions. Also, consider using a calming tone. Compare the original to the new versions to see how they change.

This exercise helps you see how important simple communication is. It's a useful way to practice talking with someone who has dementia. Normalize their experience. Say, "This seems confusing, I agree. Let's figure it out together." Lead with what you think might be happening. For example: "It seems like you're looking for something." It's often much easier for your loved one to answer yes or no questions, instead of coming up with the words themselves. "Are you looking for your keys? Are you looking for your glasses?"

THE ROLE OF BODY LANGUAGE IN COMMUNICATING

Body language is crucial in caregiving, especially with dementia. It can say so much without words, helping show empathy and understanding. Gestures, facial expressions, and posture can build a strong connection, sometimes more than words could.

Reading the Person's Body Language

Showing empathy and understanding through our natural body language is a powerful tool. Simple gestures like maintaining eye contact, a gentle touch, or especially a smile can convey support and acknowledgment. These gestures comfort the person and strengthen the bond between caregiver and recipient, building trust that will inevitably provide much better care.

Understanding a person's body language can be like learning a new dialog. It helps caregivers comprehend how the person feels and what they need. For example, if someone looks tense or avoids eye contact, they might be anxious and need reassurance or even some space. Caregivers can adjust their approach by paying attention to these cues to better meet the person's needs and improve their comfort levels. For example, If they pull or tug at their pants, they are probably trying to tell you they need to use the bathroom.

Mirroring to Build Rapport

Mirroring is like a dance where you consciously and subconsciously copy someone else's body language. It helps build a connection and makes the other person feel understood and accepted. For support providers, mirroring can be especially helpful when trying to communicate with someone with dementia. By matching their gestures or pace, caregivers show support and understanding, which can make the person feel more relaxed, inviting them to lower their guard. This shared body language helps reduce feelings of loneliness and encourages better communication.

Avoiding Intimidating Postures

Constant mindfulness of body language is crucial when interacting with dementia. Actions like standing too close or making sudden movements can make them apprehensive or even agitated. Providers should maintain a relaxed posture and distance to show respect and convey warmth. This helps prevent misunderstandings and creates a safe and positive environment for communicating. By paying attention to non-verbal cues and avoiding intimidating postures, caregivers can build a deeper connection with the person they are caring for.

TECHNIQUES TO ENHANCE UNDERSTANDING

Repeating important information and key points to reinforce understanding. Repetition can help individuals with dementia retain information. Allowing them extra time to process information and respond. Be patient and avoid rushing them. Acknowledge and validate the individual's emotions, even if their thoughts or feelings seem irrational. Show empathy and support. Provide praise and positive reinforcement for efforts to understand and communicate. Encourage and celebrate successes, no matter how small. Minimize Distractions by creating a quiet and calm environment free from distractions to help individuals focus on communication and understanding. Be flexible and adaptable in your communication approach. Experiment with different techniques to find what works best for the individual.

Using Visual Aids

Using visual aids in communicating with individuals with memory loss can greatly improve understanding when words are not enough. Pictures or physical objects can help bring back warm memories and convey messages more effectively. For example, a photo album can be a powerful tool for connection, prompting recognition and conversation. Similarly, simple icons illustrating daily schedules or instructions can sometimes guide individuals better than verbal directions, reducing confusion and empowering them to feel more independent. This approach relies on the brain's ability to process visual information, helping bridge the gap caused by dementia.

The Role of Music and Art

Music and art can deeply enrich daily functions with people living in cognitive decline. Music, with its ability to stir emotions, can evoke responses even when words fail. Familiar tunes can unlock memories and bring moments of joy, fostering connections that can reach well beyond spoken language. Likewise, art provides a medium for expression unrestricted by words, allowing individuals with dementia to communicate through color, shape, and texture. Engaging in creative activities together, like painting or crafting, becomes a shared experience where making art serves as both expression and connection. Exploring music and art as communication tools can highlight the power of creative expression, bridging the gaps and promoting understanding and connection through melody and visual storytelling.

Leveraging Technology

In today's tech-driven world, using technology to interact with those facing dementia opens up a new palette of possibilities. Tablets and smartphones, loaded with specialized apps, become valuable tools for bridging communication gaps. These apps range from fun games that stimulate the mind to necessary tools for expressing needs through pictures or icons. Video calls on these devices also allow face-to-face interactions with loved ones, boosting mood and overall engagement. Customizing these technologies to suit individual preferences and abilities makes them even more effective in maintaining interactions. Integrating technology into dementia care helps providers connect with individuals more effectively, reducing feelings of isolation.

Combining visual aids, music, art, and technology enriches the caregiver's toolbox for transmitting thoughts and ideas. These methods recognize and celebrate retained abilities. They also provide the power of nonverbal exchange, offering flexible and diverse ways to foster understanding, joy, and connection in caregiving.

ADDRESSING REPEATED ACTIVITIES, QUESTIONS AND STATEMENTS

Understanding Looping

Looping occurs when someone repeats the same gesture, says the same thing, makes the same noise, or asks the same question over and over.

In dementia care, caregivers often encounter repetitive questions, statements, and activities from those they support. While this repetition may seem trivial, it holds a deeper meaning. It reflects the need for reassurance and stability in one's rapidly changing world.

Repetition often arises from a quest for reassurance in the face of forgetfulness and uncertainty. As memories fade, repeating questions or statements becomes a way to anchor oneself in a familiar routine. Responding with patience and reassurance is crucial, as reacting with irritation only adds fuel to the anxiety. Instead, caregivers can offer understanding and compassion, providing a sense of continuity and safety.

Mastering Distraction and Redirection

You will hear this repeatedly; distraction and redirection will help break the cycle of repetition. By gently steering the conversation towards new topics or activities, caregivers can introduce variety and stimulation, enriching the individual's experience. Some simple ways are to give them easy chores to do, like folding clothes or sorting objects, play their favorite songs to make them feel happy and relaxed, offer textured items to touch or squeeze, like stress balls or soft fabrics, chat with them about happy times from their past, take short walks outside, or do some easy exercises together to help them relax and feel better. These activities can help them feel more comfortable and calm, even when they're confused or upset.

Creating Simple Routines

Establishing a comforting routine can further reduce the need for repetitive behaviors. A predictable daily structure with regular activities can decrease apprehension and provide a sense of security. Giving individuals choices within this routine enhances their autonomy and understanding of their environmental expectations.

By recognizing the underlying needs behind repetition and responding accordingly, caregivers can effectively manage this aspect of dementia care while enriching the lives of those they care for.

ADDRESSING CLINGINESS

Clinginess in dementia can stem from feelings of insecurity, fear, or discomfort. Try to understand what triggers the clinginess in the individual, such as changes in routine, unfamiliar environments, or feelings of confusion. During this time they often will exhibit a heightened need for attention, seeking reassurance, validation, and engagement from caregivers and loved ones. While managing this constant need for attention can be challenging, there are several strategies caregivers can employ to provide support and meet the individual's emotional and social needs:

- Practice Active Listening: Be present and attentive when the individual seeks attention, actively listening to their concerns, emotions, and requests. Validate their feelings and acknowledge their need for support, even if you are unable to fulfill their specific request.

- Provide Emotional Support: Offer reassurance, comfort, and empathy when the individual expresses distress or anxiety. Validate their emotions and offer words of encouragement to help alleviate their feelings of insecurity or uncertainty.

- Engage in Meaningful Activities: Plan and participate in activities that provide engagement, stimulation, and social interaction opportunities. Choose activities based on the individual's interests, hobbies, and abilities, and adapt them as needed to ensure they remain enjoyable and rewarding.

- Establish Predictable Routines: Creating daily routines and schedules, especially in a new environment, can provide structure and predictability for the individual. Consistency can help reduce anxiety and confusion, providing a sense of security and stability in their daily lives.

- Set Boundaries: While providing attention and support is important, setting boundaries is also necessary to prevent caregiver burnout and maintain your well-being. Establish clear boundaries around when and how much attention you can provide, and communicate these boundaries calmly and compassionately.

- Encourage Independence: Empower the individual to engage in activities and tasks independently to the best of their ability. Offer support and guidance as needed, but allow them to make choices and decisions independently, fostering a sense of autonomy and self-confidence.

- Utilize Distraction Techniques: Redirect the individual's attention away from negative or distressing thoughts by engaging them in a different activity or conversation. Use distraction techniques such as offering a favorite snack, listening to music, or going for a walk to shift their focus and improve their mood.
- Seek Support: Don't hesitate to reach out for support from other family members, friends, or support groups when needed. Sharing the caregiving responsibilities can help alleviate the burden of constantly meeting the individual's need for attention and provide opportunities for respite and self-care.

Breaktime for the Caregivers

Remember self-care: Taking breaks when necessary is crucial, even if it's just a brief moment to step away. Caring for someone with dementia can be draining. By following these tips, caregivers can handle the ongoing demands of caring for individuals with dementia, all while safeguarding their emotional health and preserving their own well-being and strength.

DEALING WITH HEARING PROBLEMS AND HEARING LOSS

Sound has the power to stimulate the brain, which is why hearing loss has the potential to have a profound effect on someone who has dementia. Hearing loss is associated with cognitive decline, though more research is needed to determine the degree of the connection.

The connection between hearing loss and cognitive decline is complex and varies from person to person. While it's true that some individuals who are completely deaf may not experience cognitive decline, research suggests that untreated or significant hearing loss can increase the risk of cognitive decline and conditions like dementia in some people.

Here's why:

- Sensory Stimulation: Hearing loss deprives the brain of auditory stimulation, which can lead to changes in the brain's structure and function over time. This lack of stimulation may contribute to cognitive decline.
- Cognitive Load: When individuals have difficulty hearing, their brains must work harder to interpret sounds and speech, which can lead to cognitive fatigue. This increased cognitive load may affect other cognitive functions over time.
- Social Isolation: Hearing loss can make engaging in social activities and maintaining social connections challenging, leading to social isolation. Social isolation is a known risk factor for cognitive decline and dementia.
- Brain Structure Changes: Studies have shown that untreated hearing loss is associated with changes in brain structure, including reduced gray matter volume in speech and auditory processing areas. These structural changes may contribute to cognitive decline.
- Shared Risk Factors: Some risk factors for hearing loss, such as cardiovascular disease and diabetes, are also associated with cognitive decline. Thus, individuals with these shared risk factors may be at increased risk for hearing loss and cognitive decline.

While some people with hearing loss may not experience cognitive decline, it's essential to recognize that hearing loss can be a contributing factor for others. Managing hearing loss through interventions like hearing aids and maintaining overall brain health through activities such as cognitive stimulation and social engagement can help mitigate the risk of cognitive decline associated with hearing loss.

WHAT NOT TO DO

- Do not tell them they are wrong about anything.
- Don't correct them.
- Do not argue with them.
- Do not ask if they remember something.
- Do not remind them that their spouse, parent, or other loved one is deceased.
- Do not bring up topics that could obviously upset them.

CHAPTER 3

NAVIGATING PERSONALITY AND BEHAVIORAL CHANGES

S omeone with dementia can have rapid mood swings, for no apparent reason. Behavioral changes can be puzzling for the individual and those caring for them. These changes, like agitation or withdrawal, are not random; they reflect the brain's struggle to cope with its changed condition. By properly understanding and interpreting these changes, caregivers can transform frustrating moments into opportunities for connection and improved care.

UNDERSTANDING THE CAUSES OF BEHAVIORAL CHANGES

Environmental factors, physical discomfort, and communication breakdowns can often act as a catalyst for behavioral changes in individuals with dementia. Like a stone thrown into a still pond, the ripples of these triggers can disturb the relative peace of a person's demeanor. For instance, an overly loud TV can be the stone that unsettles the water, leading to agitation. Recognizing these triggers requires keen observation and a willingness to adjust the environment to suit the individual's evolving needs. They are often simply looking for something to do with their hands. Making a rummage box for them to sort through will keep their hands busy.

The Role of Disease Progression

As dementia progresses, the brain undergoes significant alterations, affecting behavior. This progression can lead to an increased frequency and intensity of more challenging behaviors. It's akin to a path becoming more treacherous as one walks further along; the journey becomes more difficult to navigate, and the likelihood of stumbling grows. Understanding this correlation between disease progression and behavioral changes is crucial for setting realistic expectations and planning care strategies.

Emotional Underpinnings

The emotional distress and confusion that often underlie changes in behavior will point toward the unmet needs of individuals with dementia. These behaviors are expressions of an internal struggle, a way of communicating discomfort or dissatisfaction when verbal exchange fails. Imagine being in a foreign country, unable to speak the language, and trying to express your needs. The frustration that would ensue is similar to what those afflicted with dementia experience, leading them to communicate through behaviors instead of words.

Misinterpretation of Behaviors

A common misstep is viewing challenging behaviors as deliberate negative actions rather than expressions of unmet needs. This misinterpretation can lead to more punitive than supportive responses, exacerbating the situation. A helpful analogy is mistaking a cry for help as a call to arms; the reaction it provokes is likely to be defensive rather than compassionate. Shifting perception to view these behaviors as attempts at communication encourages a more empathetic and practical caregiving approach. These outbursts are referred to as responsive behavior, indicating that there is a reason behind the behavior. This happens usually in the middle and late stages of dementia.

Strategies for Addressing Common Responsive Behaviors

Encouraging communication is crucial when responding to behaviors in individuals with dementia. It may take some time to find the most effective strategy. Here's how caregivers can ask them to express their needs:

- Use Simple Language: Speak in simple, clear sentences and avoid using complicated language. This makes it easier for the individual to understand and respond.
- Ask Questions: Encourage the person to express themselves. For example, instead of asking, "Do you want something to eat?" try asking, "What would you like to eat?"
- Provide Visual Cues: Use visual cues or gestures to help the individual communicate their needs. Point to objects or pictures that represent common needs, such as food, water, or the restroom.
- Offer Choices: Provide the person with choices to help them express their preferences. For example, you can say, "Would you like tea or coffee?" or "Do you want to go for a walk or sit outside?"
- Be Patient: Give the person plenty of time to respond. Avoid rushing or interrupting them while they're trying to communicate.

- Use Nonverbal Communication: Pay attention to the individual's nonverbal cues, such as facial expressions, gestures, or body language. These can provide valuable clues about their needs and preferences.
- Validate Their Efforts: Acknowledge and validate the person's attempts to communicate, even if they're not able to express themselves clearly. Let them know that you're listening and trying to understand them.
- Offer Assistance: If the person is having difficulty expressing their needs verbally, offer alternative methods of communication, such as writing, drawing, or using communication aids.
- Create a Calm Environment: Ensure that the environment is calm and free from distractions to help the individual focus on communicating their needs.

Visual Elements: Checklist for Identifying Triggers

This checklist is a practical tool for caregivers. It helps pinpoint potential triggers for behavioral changes and covers environmental, physical, and communicative aspects, offering a structured way to assess and adjust the care environment to mitigate these triggers.

- Loud and crowded places that overstimulate the senses
- Unfamiliar faces, including too many attendants
- Environmental changes, such as relocating or visiting strange places
- Hunger or thirst
- Needing to use the restroom
- Sudden unforeseen approaches
- Loud forceful communication

- The invasion of private space
- Misunderstanding conversations or questions
- Startling loud noises and voices
- Uncomfortable room temperatures
- Feeling demeaned or disrespected
- Being bored or feeling lonely
- In pain or discomfort
- Having an infection like a UTI
- Side effects and reactions to medications

Pain itself is a significant trigger of behavioral disturbance but is often overlooked or ignored. Common complaints concern musculoskeletal pain such as joint, back, and leg pain. Understanding behavioral changes in dementia is crucial for providers.

Using this checklist, care providers can create a more supportive environment, reduce the frequency of behavioral challenges, and enhance the well-being of individuals with dementia.

STRATEGIES FOR MANAGING AGITATION AND AGGRESSION

Dealing with agitation and aggression in dementia care can be difficult, but it's possible to navigate these challenges with calm, understanding, and safety-focused strategies. Caregivers can turn these moments into peace and connection by prioritizing serenity and empathy. Don't try to reason with them or push them to do something. Instead, try to find ways to engage them as they are now. Simple activities such as listening to music, sorting or stacking objects, or going for a walk or a car ride are good options.

Non-Confrontational Approach

The key to handling agitation and aggression is to remain calm and patient rather than reacting defensively. Instead of engaging in confrontation, it is important to understand the underlying cause of the distress and address it with empathy and serenity. By maintaining a peaceful demeanor, caregivers can help restore a sense of calm and prevent further escalation of agitation or aggression.

Simple phrases like "I can see this is tough for you" or "Let's figure this out together" show support and understanding. This kind of communication can help bring the person back to a calmer state by letting them know they're understood and respected.

Environmental Adjustments

The places we spend time in are not just backgrounds; they can affect how we feel. For people with dementia, too much noise or clutter can be overwhelming and make them feel anxious. To help, we should design spaces with care. This might include using softer lighting, reducing loud noises, or tidying up to avoid overwhelming them. These changes create calm environments that respect their limits and help them feel more comfortable.

Personal Safety

During times of dementia-related aggression, the top priority is keeping everyone safe. Caregivers should focus on protecting themselves as well as the person in need. This might mean keeping a safe distance, making sure there is a clear way to leave the room if needed, or using gentle holds if safety is at risk. They should also check the environment for anything that could be harmful, like objects with sharp edges or that could be thrown. Knowing when to ask for extra help from healthcare professionals or emergency services is important too. This focus on safety is not about seeing the person as dangerous but understanding that dementia can cause unpredictable behavior. It's about making sure everyone stays safe while facing the challenges of aggressive behavior.

Dealing with agitation and aggression can be complex in dementia care. However, caregivers can turn these challenges into opportunities by using strategies like non-confrontational approaches, adjusting the environment, using effective communication, and always keeping safety in mind. Keep eye contact and try to explain calmly why you are there. Gently encourage the person to communicate with you. If you are trying to support the person with an activity or task, consider whether it needs to be done now. If you are able to, give them space, come back later and try again. Focus on the person, not the behavior. Even after the behavior has passed, the person may still feel upset and distressed, even if they have forgotten what happened or what they were responding to. Try to be as reassuring as possible.

If the behavior continues, you may have to consider placing the person in a memory care facility. These facilities have staff trained in dementia care who can help manage aggression and keep residents calm.

DEALING WITH WANDERING SAFELY

Wandering is not just wandering; it is a search driven by various reasons that might be confusing to outsiders. It can stem from simple boredom, restlessness, or a desire to find something familiar from the past. Despite the risks involved, it highlights the person's need for activity and connection, prompting caregivers to balance these needs with safety concerns.

Safety Measures in the Home

Creating a safe environment is essential for individuals living with dementia to navigate their daily lives with confidence and comfort, from minimizing hazards to promoting independence.

Here are some enhanced wandering safety tips:

- Install Door Sensors: Consider installing door sensors or alarms that sound when exterior doors are opened. These devices can alert caregivers or family members if the person attempts to leave the house unaccompanied.
- Utilize GPS Tracking Devices: Explore using GPS tracking devices, such as wearable GPS bracelets or pendants, to monitor a person's whereabouts in real-time. This technology can help quickly locate them if they wander away from home.
- Create a Safe Outdoor Space: If the person enjoys spending time outdoors, create a secure outdoor area with fencing or gates to prevent them from wandering beyond the yard. Ensure that the outdoor space is free of hazards and has comfortable seating and shade.
- Implement Routine and Structure: Establishing a consistent daily routine and schedule can help reduce restlessness and wandering behaviors. Engage the person in meaningful activities and provide regular meals, rest periods, and opportunities for exercise.
- Consider Identifying Clothing: Sew labels with the person's name and contact information into their clothing or attach identification tags to their shoes or belongings. This can be helpful if they become lost and someone needs to assist them.

- Provide Engaging Activities: Keep the person occupied with stimulating activities that capture their interest and attention. Activities like puzzles, crafts, music, or gardening can help redirect their energy and reduce the likelihood of wandering.
- Communicate with Neighbors and Community Members: Inform neighbors, local businesses, and community members about the person's dementia diagnosis and wandering tendencies. Provide them with contact information in case the person is found wandering outside the home.
- Seek Professional Support: Consult with healthcare professionals, including physicians, social workers, or dementia specialists, for additional guidance and support in managing wandering behaviors. They can offer personalized strategies and resources based on the individual's needs.

By incorporating these additional safety measures and strategies, caregivers can better ensure the well-being and security of individuals with dementia who may be prone to wandering.

Technology Aids

Technology offers promising avenues for enhancing dementia care by providing innovative solutions to address various challenges faced by individuals living with the condition and their caregivers. From GPS tracking devices to reminder apps and virtual reality therapy, technological advancements continue to revolutionize how we support and assist those affected by dementia. By leveraging technology, caregivers can access tools and resources to improve safety, communication, cognitive stimulation, and quality of life for individuals with dementia.

Embracing these technological innovations can empower caregivers and enable individuals with dementia to live more independently and comfortably in their homes and communities.

Creating a Safe Wandering Path

A thoughtful approach to dealing with wandering in dementia care involves creating safe paths for movement. This means setting up secure areas indoors or outdoors where individuals can walk freely without getting lost or hurt. These paths are carefully designed, free of obstacles, and enriched with calming features like benches and gardens. They provide a safe outlet for wandering while stimulating the senses and nurturing memory and recognition. Benches or chairs may inspire the alternative to sit down instead of wander.

TECHNIQUES FOR REDUCING ANXIETY AND DEPRESSION

In dementia's world, anxiety and depression are common and troubling companions. They stem from the confusion and loss that come with the disease. This is when you might notice them hoarding, hiding, or losing things. Redirect their attention to something pleasurable. Many times, hoarding demonstrates a need for comfort because of deep fears and anxiety. Don't try to use logic because it will not be effective. Be compassionate and understand that the hoarding is a response to dementia. You will need to keep important things in a safe and undisclosed place that they cannot reach. Caregivers must recognize these feelings and work to ease them, using strategies that promote emotional well-being and peace of mind.

Activity Engagement

Engaging in meaningful activities is powerful in combating anxiety and depression. Individuals find comfort and relief by doing things that resonate with their interests and abilities. For example, a former gardener may enjoy the feel of soil, while a musician may find solace in playing familiar tunes or instruments. Individuals with dementia may engage in various behaviors that provide them with comfort, stimulation, or a sense of familiarity. Holding a baby doll is one such behavior that is commonly observed in individuals with dementia. Here are some other activities or behaviors that people with dementia may engage in:

- Fidgeting or Pacing: Restlessness, fidgeting with objects, or pacing back and forth may occur due to anxiety, agitation, or the need for sensory stimulation.
- Sorting or Organizing Objects: Some individuals with dementia may enjoy sorting or organizing objects, such as arranging items on a table or categorizing household items.
- Talking to Themselves: Engaging in self-talk or having conversations with imaginary companions is a common behavior observed in individuals with dementia. It may serve as a way to express thoughts or feelings or provide companionship.
- Repetitive Actions or Gestures: Repeatedly performing the same actions, such as tapping fingers, clapping hands, or rubbing surfaces, can be a manifestation of cognitive impairment and may provide sensory stimulation or comfort.
- Hoarding or Hiding Objects: Collecting and hoarding objects or hiding items in unusual places may result in

confusion, memory loss, or a need to maintain a sense of control.

- Engaging in Personal Care Routines: Some individuals with dementia may maintain personal care routines, such as brushing their hair, folding clothes, or grooming themselves, as these activities provide them with a sense of familiarity and routine.
- Engaging with Pets: Interacting with pets, such as stroking a cat or talking to a dog, can provide comfort, companionship, and sensory stimulation for individuals with dementia.
- Engaging in Creative Activities: Painting, drawing, crafting, or engaging in other creative activities may provide individuals with dementia with a sense of purpose, accomplishment, and enjoyment.
- Watching Familiar TV Shows or Movies: Viewing familiar TV shows, movies, or family photos can evoke memories, spark conversation, and provide individuals with dementia with a sense of connection to their past.
- Engaging in Music or Singing: Listening to music, singing along to familiar songs, or playing musical instruments can elicit emotional responses, trigger memories, and provide individuals with dementia with comfort and enjoyment.

Social Interaction

Building connections with others is crucial for combatting feelings of isolation, especially in dementia. Even though cognitive decline and social withdrawal pose challenges, it's essential to create opportunities for interaction. Simple activities like having meals together and reminiscing about the past can offer support and help them feel and stay connected, easing the burden of anxiety and depression in a world that may seem unfamiliar.

Physical Exercise

Regular physical exercise, tailored to fit the individual's abilities and preferences, isn't just good for the body—it's great for emotional health too. Activities like walking, aquatic therapy, or tai chi can help ease anxiety and depression by providing a healthy outlet for pent-up energy. Plus, exercise releases feel-good chemicals in the body and improves sleep quality, which can help counteract the biochemical factors behind these emotional challenges. So, exercise isn't just about staying fit—it's a holistic approach to promoting strength and peace of mind for those dealing with dementia.

Professional Support

Recognizing the need for professional help is crucial when dealing with anxiety and depression in dementia. These emotional states, while common, may require more than just everyday interventions. Seeking support from counselors, psychiatrists, or therapists who understand dementia can provide tailored treatments. This collaborative approach ensures a comprehensive response to emotional challenges, valuing mental well-being as much as physical health.

Managing anxiety and depression in dementia requires a mix of strategies, such as staying active, socializing, exercising, and seeking professional help. Each plays a role in addressing the emotional complexities of dementia. By using these strategies with care and compassion, caregivers can provide comfort and guidance through the emotional ups and downs. It's a reminder that in dementia care, emotional and physical health go hand in hand, and both deserve attention and care.

HOW TO HANDLE INAPPROPRIATE BEHAVIORS

Understanding dementia means knowing how it can cause strange or troubling behaviors. As a person's dementia progresses, they may sometimes behave in ways that are physically or verbally aggressive. This can be very distressing for the person and those around them. Caregivers must respond with care and kindness while keeping safety and dignity in mind.

Setting Boundaries

Setting boundaries is highly important in caregiving. It's not about being strict but rather creating a safe and clear structure for the person with dementia. Boundaries help them know what is okay and what is not. For instance, caregivers can kindly explain that while feeling frustrated is okay, shouting might upset others. This conversation helps the person understand how their actions affect others and encourages better behavior. Maintain consistency in enforcing boundaries and consequences for aggressive behaviors. Clearly communicate expectations and follow through with appropriate responses when boundaries are crossed.

Here's an example of how you could communicate this boundary:

"Hey [Name], I understand you may be feeling upset right now, but it's not okay to hurt me. I want to help you, but I must keep both of us safe. If you're feeling upset or frustrated, let's try to find a different way to express it. How about we take a walk or sit down and talk about what's bothering you? I care about you and want us both to feel safe and respected."

This example acknowledges the individual's feelings while firmly asserting the boundary that hurting others is not acceptable. It offers alternative ways to address their emotions and encourages open communication to address the underlying issues.

Distraction and Redirection

You may find that distraction and redirection techniques are often repeated as ways to handle many situations because they are invaluable tools when enforcing boundaries doesn't work. Caregivers adeptly redirect the individual's attention to alternative activities or interests. For instance, when faced with a desire to wander alone outdoors, a caregiver might gently suggest a leisurely stroll in the garden together or engage the individual in a purposeful task such as folding laundry. This shift in focus keeps them safe while satisfying their need for activity and purpose, providing opportunities to feel helpful and relevant, and turning challenging situations into positive moments.

Understanding the Behavior's Origin

To understand and address inappropriate behaviors in dementia, caregivers need to look beyond the surface and uncover the reasons behind them. Rather than seeing these actions as intentional, they should view them as signs of need or discomfort. This involves patiently observing and listening to the person. For example, if someone undresses in public, it might be because they feel too hot or uncomfortable. By understanding this, providers can address the root cause by ensuring the person wears lighter clothes. Based on empathy and understanding, this approach respects the person's dignity and creates a caring environment that meets their needs.

ENCOURAGING POSITIVE BEHAVIOR WITH REINFORCEMENT

In dementia caregiving, encouraging positive behaviors through praise and recognition is absolutely crucial. This method, based on the idea that rewarded behavior is likely to continue, provides a very helpful strategy. By praising and encouraging behaviors that improve well-being and social interactions, caregivers can create a positive environment where everyone benefits.

Positive Reinforcement

Positive reinforcement is about recognizing and rewarding good behaviors promptly. This could be as simple as giving verbal praise, a smile, or even a small gift. It taps into our basic need for acknowledgment and belonging, encouraging people to repeat positive actions. For someone with dementia, moments of clarity and connection can be rare, but when they happen, praising them right away can make them feel capable and valued. This method isn't just about changing behavior; it is about lifting the person up and celebrating their achievements, no matter how small, in the midst of their struggles with memory loss.

Celebrating Small Successes

In dementia care, even small wins matter greatly. Celebrating these victories – like a clear moment, a calm day, or a sweet gesture – is key to positive reinforcement. By acknowledging and appreciating these moments, caregivers boost the individual's confidence and encourage more of these positive behaviors. Ways to celebrate these successes might include sharing a favorite treat, expressing heartfelt gratitude, and creating a visual representation of achievements, like a wall of fame, that the individual and their family can see.

Consistency Is Key

The effectiveness of using positive reinforcement relies on how consistently it's used. When caregivers consistently respond positively to good behavior, it creates a dependable system that the individual can understand and rely on. This consistency isn't just about the caregiver – it involves the whole care team. By everyone being on the same page, positive behaviors are recognized and rewarded across the board, making them even more desirable. This means everyone involved in the person's care needs to communicate and work together. This unified effort sends a strong message that good behavior is valued and appreciated. It encourages more of the same behavior and builds a strong support system around the individual, making sure they feel encouraged and supported in their actions.

SIGNS OF SOMEONE SUDDENLY WORSENING

A sudden deterioration or change in behavior, cognition, or physical function can often be a sign that an underlying health issue is taking place, for individuals living with dementia. One concern is the onset of delirium, which can be triggered by infections such as urinary tract infections (UTIs), respiratory infections, or other systemic illnesses. Delirium can manifest as confusion, agitation, or changes in consciousness and may exacerbate existing dementia symptoms.

Moreover, sudden changes such as a stroke may signal a cerebrovascular event. Strokes can occur due to disruptions in blood flow to the brain, leading to neurological deficits that can mimic or exacerbate dementia symptoms. This is particularly common in certain types of vascular dementia, where the brain's blood vessels are damaged or impaired, increasing the risk of stroke. In some cases, strokes can occur in a series of "steps," each causing further deterioration in cognitive and functional abilities.

Therefore, caregivers and healthcare professionals must be vigilant and proactive in monitoring sudden changes in individuals with dementia. Prompt medical assessment and intervention can help identify underlying causes, such as infections or strokes, potentially preventing further decline and improving the individual's overall quality of life.

When sudden changes occur in the decline of someone's health with dementia, it is essential to take swift action to address the situation. Here are some things you can do:

- Assess the Situation: It is vital to observe the person closely, noting any new symptoms or behaviors that have emerged, to determine the nature and extent of the changes.
- Check for Immediate Needs: Ensure the person's immediate requirements, such as safety, comfort, and hydration, are met.
- Contact Healthcare Professionals: Contact the individual's healthcare team, including their primary care physician or specialist, to report the changes and seek guidance on the next steps.
- Seek Medical Evaluation: Arrange for the person to receive a prompt medical assessment to determine the underlying cause of the sudden decline. Depending on the severity of the situation, this may involve visiting a doctor's office, urgent care facility, or emergency room.
- Provide Comfort and Support: Offer reassurance and emotional support to the person with dementia during this challenging time. Maintain a calm and comforting

presence to help alleviate any distress they may be experiencing.

- Update Care Plan: Work with healthcare professionals to update the person's care plan based on the new developments. This may involve medication adjustments, interventions to address specific symptoms, or additional support services.

- Communicate with Family and Caregivers: It is essential to keep family members and other caregivers fully informed about the situation and any changes to the person's condition or care plan. This collaborative approach ensures a coordinated response to providing adequate support and assistance.

- Monitor Progress: Continuously monitor the person's condition and response to treatment, and follow up with healthcare professionals as needed to address any ongoing concerns or complications.

- Take Care of Yourself: Remember to prioritize your well-being as a care provider. Seek support from family, friends, or support groups to help you cope with the challenges of caring for someone with dementia during times of sudden health changes.

APPROACHES TO ADDRESSING SUNDOWNING

The phenomenon of sundowning, where the cloak of the evening shifts toward increased confusion, restlessness, and agitation in individuals with dementia, requires a nuanced approach. This pattern, as predictable as the setting sun yet fraught with unpredictability in its manifestation, challenges caregivers to adapt their strategies as day transitions into night. Understanding this phenomenon's complex interplay with the circadian rhythm and the brain's altered processing in dementia is the first step toward mitigating its impact.

Recognizing Sundowning Symptoms

Recognizing sundowning is like sensing an approaching storm. As daylight fades, symptoms like confusion, anxiety, and agitation may worsen, especially in the evening. Caregivers must be vigilant during this time, watching for signs and being ready to help the individual. It's a challenging period when the peacefulness of the day can turn into chaos, affecting both the person with sundowning and their care providers.

Environmental Modifications

Adjusting the environment to ease sundowning involves carefully managing light and sound. As daylight fades, increasing indoor lighting can help create a comforting atmosphere, preventing shadows that may cause confusion. At the same time, reducing noise can prevent sensory overload and agitation. Lowering the volume of electronics and choosing quieter activities in the evening can help create a peaceful environment that supports a smooth transition from day to night. Having pictures and things that are familiar to them can reassure them that they are in a safe place.

Routine and Schedule Adjustments

A structured daily routine is essential for individuals with dementia, especially when dealing with sundowning. Following a predictable sequence of activities throughout the day helps anchor the individual and reduces disorientation. A calming evening routine and relaxing activities like listening to soft music or gentle stretching can be particularly helpful. Keeping the day filled with engaging activities also helps prevent late-day naps, which can worsen sundowning symptoms. Once the routine is established, it becomes a comforting pattern that eases the transition into the night.

Medication Management

While non-drug methods are the main approach for dealing with sundowning, medication can sometimes be helpful with careful supervision from a healthcare professional. Medication aims to address specific symptoms like sleep problems or anxiety that can make sundowning worse. Careful consideration of any medication's benefits and potential side effects is important. The goal is to improve the individual's quality of life without too much affecting their clarity and presence. Medication is just one part of a broader plan that respects the individual's needs and well-being.

Caregivers use a combination of strategies, such as adjusting the environment and creating a structured routine, to manage sundowning. When needed, medication is part of this plan. These efforts aim to create a calm environment in the evening, helping individuals with dementia feel more peaceful. Providers show their support by ensuring every moment is met with care and understanding.

UNDERSTANDING PARANOID EPISODES AND HALLUCINATIONS

Paranoia is a type of delusion in which someone believes without good reason that others are lying or out to get them. Delusions are false beliefs that aren't real. For example, they may become suspicious of you or others, accusing someone is stealing, or think their spouse is still alive. Hallucinations are when someone sees, hears, smells, or even feels things that are not really there. If someone has hallucinations, stay with them and try to reassure them. Hallucinations may be limited to a particular setting. Gently leading someone away from where they are can help make them disappear.

Here are some tips for coping with paranoia, hallucinations and delusions:

- Try not to react if the person blames you for something.
- Try not to argue with the person about what they are seeing or hearing.
- Redirect their attention, using gentle touch or hugging with their permission.
- Turn off the TV when violent or upsetting programs are on.
- Try to distract them or get them to move to another area.
- Discuss with the doctor any illnesses and medications they are taking.

CHAPTER 4

SUPPORTING DAILY LIFE

During twilight, helping someone with dementia with personal hygiene can turn into a quiet connection of care. Simple actions like brushing hair or washing hands become a way of showing respect and reinforcing trust. In these quiet moments, the true meaning of caregiving shines through, showing it is more than just tasks—it is about treating each other with dignity. However, mood disruptions are quite common in all stages of dementia progression, and some are more serious than others. This can limit their ability to do daily tasks like shopping, cooking, showering, dressing, or paying their bills.

ASSISTING WITH PERSONAL HYGIENE AND CARE

Empowering Independence

For someone with dementia, being able to care for themselves is like keeping parts of their life story alive. Each time they can wash, dress, or groom themselves, it is like adding a new chapter to their book, showing who they are and what they like. Helping them stay independent means finding ways to support them while letting them keep control. Small changes, like using pictures on toiletry labels or choosing easy-to-wear clothes, can make a big difference in helping them take care of themselves. This independence is a powerful way to show them they are still valued for who they are.

But there comes a time when the sequence of things like brushing their teeth becomes confusing. This is when you can help them understand by having them mirror you. It's like teaching a child to brush their teeth for the first time; you actually show them how it's done by doing it with them.

Sensitive Assistance

Helping with personal hygiene requires being sensitive to the person's vulnerability. It's about understanding that tasks like touching their skin or combing their hair can feel intimate. Communication is key, so explaining each step calmly and respectfully is important. Asking for their permission before doing anything and respecting their choices turns routine care into a way to show mutual respect. Making eye contact, giving options, and using caring gestures all help create an environment where their dignity is valued, and they feel appreciated and heard.

Adapting Hygiene Routines

- Breaking down tasks into more straightforward steps/letting them mirror you.
- Using visual aids to guide the process.
- Adjusting the timing of routines to align with their most lucid moments of the day.

For instance, a bath might transition to a supervised sponge bath, reducing the risk of falls while still achieving the goal of cleanliness. Each carefully considered and executed adjustment underscores a commitment to providing respectful and responsive care.

Use of Assistive Devices

Assistive devices play a crucial role in the symphony of caregiving, amplifying efforts to maintain safety and independence in personal care. Devices such as grab bars in the shower, non-slip mats, and adapted toilet seats become instrumental in creating a safe environment. They act not as crutches but as empowerment tools, enabling individuals to navigate their hygiene routines with greater confidence and autonomy.

Caring for someone with dementia, especially when it comes to bathing and feeding, requires patience, compassion, and sensitivity to their needs and preferences. Here are some practical tips for handling these caregiving tasks:

Practical Bathing Tips

- Establish a Routine: Create a consistent bathing schedule to help your loved one feel more comfortable and secure. Stick to the same time of day and follow a predictable sequence of steps to minimize confusion.
- Prepare the Environment: Ensure the bathroom is warm, well-lit, and free from clutter. Consider installing grab bars, non-slip mats, and handheld showerheads for added safety and convenience.
- Provide Clear Instructions: Use simple, step-by-step instructions and verbal cues to guide your loved one

through bathing. Break down tasks into manageable steps and offer reassurance and encouragement along the way.

- Respect Privacy and Dignity: Maintain your loved one's privacy by closing doors and using towels or bathrobes to cover exposed areas. Respect their preferences regarding who assists with bathing and provide choices whenever possible.
- Use Gentle Touch: Handle your loved one with care and gentleness, using a soothing and reassuring tone of voice. Be mindful of any physical limitations or discomfort they may experience, and adjust your approach accordingly.
- Consider Sponge Baths: If your loved one is resistant to traditional baths or showers, consider offering sponge baths as an alternative. This can be a more comfortable and less overwhelming option for some individuals with dementia.
- Offer Distractions: Provide comforting distractions during bathing, such as favorite music, calming scents, or engaging conversation. This can help redirect their focus and reduce anxiety or agitation.
- Be Flexible: Be prepared to adapt your approach based on your loved one's response and needs. If they are resistant to bathing on a particular day, try again later or explore alternative methods of maintaining hygiene, such as dry shampoo or washcloths.

Help with Using the Bathroom at Home

- Help the person identify where the toilet is by putting a sign on the door, including both words and a picture. The sign needs to be bright and easy to see.

- Check the position of the mirrors in the bathroom. The person with dementia may confuse their reflection for someone else and not go because they think someone else is in there.
- The bathroom and the route to it should be well-lit, especially at night, to help people find their way.
- Some struggle with the locks. To prevent them from locking themselves in, disable the locks and ensure that you are able to open the door quickly from the outside.
- Choose clothing that is easier for the person to undo when using the toilet. Consider clothing with Velcro fastenings.
- Men may find it easier to sit when they are less mobile or their balance is difficult. Handrails and a raised toilet seat will help as well.
- You can use a bedside commode if getting to the toilet becomes too difficult.

Excessive Toilet Paper Usage

Numerous factors contribute to increased toilet paper consumption among individuals with dementia. Common reasons are forgetfulness regarding its purpose, the urge to clean up accidents, confusion regarding appropriate usage, and the development of compulsive behaviors. Additionally, some dementia patients face challenges with motor skills, making it difficult to tear off an appropriate amount, while changes in perception and sensory processing may alter their perceived need for paper.

Caregivers should vigilantly monitor toilet paper usage and address underlying issues. This may involve implementing strategies for managing incontinence, providing assistance with toileting, or establishing reminders and routines to promote proper hygiene practices.

Coping with Incontinence

Accidents and incontinence can cause problems, especially as a person's condition progresses. When the person loses the ability to recognize the need to go to the bathroom or be able to wait until an appropriate time to go, can be upsetting and difficult, but there are tools to help you cope and maintain dignity. Provide a reminder to use the bathroom just before his or her usual time. Try setting a regular schedule for toilet use. For example, help the person to the bathroom first thing in the morning, every two hours during the day, immediately after meals, and just before bedtime.

There are several types of urinary incontinence. One of these, especially common in people with dementia is an overactive bladder. This causes the feeling of a sudden and intense need to pee and frequent peeing. Women are also at particular risk of urinary incontinence when they cough, sneeze, or laugh, caused by childbirth. Fecal incontinence can range from accidentally leaking a small amount of poo when breaking wind to having no bowel control at all. Fecal incontinence is less common than urinary incontinence.

Incontinence occurs when the communication between the brain and the bladder or bowel malfunctions, leading to difficulties in recognizing fullness or controlling bodily functions. Various factors contribute to this, including:

- Delayed response to the sensation of needing to use the toilet.
- Inability to reach the toilet in time, often due to limited mobility.

- Challenges in communicating the need to use the toilet.
- Difficulty understanding prompts to use the toilet from others.
- Confusion leading to urination or defecation in inappropriate locations.
- Difficulty with tasks necessary for using the toilet, such as undressing.
- Reluctance to accept assistance with toileting, possibly due to embarrassment or misunderstanding.
- Lack of motivation or distraction prevents attempts to locate the toilet.
- Embarrassment after an accident, which the person unsuccessfully tries to manage. For example, they may try to hide wet or soiled clothes at the back of a drawer to deal with later, and then forget they've put them there.

Medical causes of incontinence include:

- Urinary tract infection (UTI) and constipation are uncomfortable and make emptying and controlling the bladder more difficult.
- Constipation is also a very common cause of fecal incontinence. Taking a stool softener regularly is beneficial.
- Side effects of medication: The GP may be able to address these by changing the person's prescription or altering the dose.
- Irritable bowel syndrome (IBS).
- Prostate gland problems – These affect men and may be treatable.

Their doctor should review the symptoms and any underlying medical conditions such as urinary tract infection or constipation, diet, or medications that might be causing the problems. You may have to be persistent until they get relief. Making simple changes to lifestyle, such as diet, drinks, and exercise, can help to achieve better results.

For some, the focus will be on managing the incontinence as comfortably as possible by using aids like incontinence pads and pull-up pants, which can be worn day and night. It's important to find the right type and absorbency for the person. The pads should be comfortable without chafing the skin or leaking and should be changed as often as necessary.

An absorbent bed pad is an undersheet that provides a dry surface on a bed or a chair. It is available as a washable or disposable product. A waterproof mattress protector is often used in combination with an absorbent bed pad. The protector should not come into contact with the skin, as it may cause chafing and soreness. You can also buy special protective duvet covers and pillowcases

Maintaining a Healthy Bladder and Bowls

Tips for keeping the bladder, urinary tract, and bowels healthy are a good first step in preventing toilet problems and incontinence.

- Encourage them to drink six to eight glasses of liquids each day.
- Ensure they eat a balanced diet with plenty of fruit and vegetables.
- Walking will help with regular bowel movements.
- Build a bathroom schedule into the person's routine and allow enough time for them to empty their bowels.

SIMPLIFYING DRESSING AND CLOTHING CHOICES

Dressing, a routine we often take for granted, is essential in dementia care. It is not just about picking clothes but about affirming the person's identity and independence. Caregivers need to handle this carefully, ensuring it helps the person feel involved while honoring their clothing preferences over the years.

Choosing Appropriate Clothing

Choosing comfortable and easy-to-wear clothes is essential, but it is also crucial to consider the person's history and tastes. Clothes that are both comfortable and stylish can boost morale and help maintain the person's identity despite the challenges of memory impairment. Clothing with elastic waists and Velcro closures makes dressing easier and gives the person more independence while allowing them to express their own choices in color, texture, and design. The key is to create a wardrobe that respects the person's past preferences—like bright colors or soft fabrics—while meeting their current needs. This balance ensures that getting dressed remains a way to express oneself rather than a reminder of limitations.

Organizing the Wardrobe

An organized, thoughtfully arranged wardrobe empowers individuals to participate in dressing to the best of their abilities. Strategies such as arranging clothes in order of dressing or grouping outfits simplify the process, reducing decision fatigue and potential frustration. Labeling drawers with words or pictures depicting their contents can guide the individual more intuitively toward making a choice.

There might be a time when they forget which order underwear and clothing go on first. They might put the underwear on the outside of their clothing. Although this will make you laugh, it indicates that things are getting more challenging for them. This is where a mirror can help, watching themselves get dressed might take some confusion out of the process.

Adaptive Clothing Options

Innovation in adaptive clothing has opened new avenues for individuals with dementia, offering garments that address the specific challenges posed by mobility issues or sensory sensitivities. These clothing options, designed with discreet modifications such as magnetic closures instead of buttons or side-open trousers to accommodate mobility aids, ensure that dressing does not become a battleground for independence. Introducing such clothing to the individual's wardrobe is an exercise in subtlety and sensitivity, ensuring that the garments align with their aesthetic styles and the narrative of their past, thus preserving their dignity. Adaptive clothing, in its essence, is not about altering the individual to fit the clothes but reimagining the clothes to fit the individual's life, ensuring that dignity, style, and comfort remain intertwined in the fabric of daily living.

NUTRITIONAL NEEDS AND MANAGING MEALS

Eating goes beyond just filling the stomach; it is vital for keeping the brain healthy, especially for dementia patients. The relationship between food and the brain is complex, with each nutrient either supporting mental function or leaving it vulnerable. A well-rounded diet, full of vitamins, minerals, and antioxidants, is like fuel for the brain, protecting memory and thinking skills. Omega-3 fatty acids in fish help strengthen brain connections, while vitamins in colorful fruits and vegetables support cognitive health. Together in a balanced diet, these nutrients offer hope for maintaining mental well-being.

Brain Foods for Cognitive Function

Fatty Fish: Rich in omega-3 fatty acids, particularly EPA and DHA, fatty fish like Salmon, Mackerel, Tuna, and Sardines are essential for brain health. These fatty acids support brain structure and function, improve memory, and can help support cognitive care.

Leafy Greens: Leafy green vegetables such as Spinach, Kale, Collard Greens, and Swiss Chard are packed with vitamins (like folate, vitamin K, and vitamin C), minerals (such as iron and calcium), and antioxidants (like lutein and zeaxanthin) that promote brain health and cognitive function.

Berries: Blueberries, Strawberries, Blackberries, and Raspberries are rich in antioxidants known as flavonoids, which have been linked to improved cognitive function, memory, and learning. Berries are also high in vitamin C, which helps protect brain cells from oxidative stress.

Nuts and Seeds: Almonds, Walnuts, Cashews, Flaxseeds, and Chia seeds are excellent sources of healthy fats, vitamins, minerals (like magnesium and zinc), and antioxidants. These nutrients support brain function, improve memory, and may help reduce the risk of cognitive decline.

Whole Grains: Whole grains like Oats, Quinoa, Brown rice, and whole wheat are rich in fiber, vitamins (such as B vitamins), minerals (like magnesium and iron), and antioxidants. They provide a steady source of energy to the brain and support overall cognitive health.

Avocados: Avocados are packed with healthy monounsaturated fats, vitamins (including vitamin K, vitamin E, and folate), and antioxidants like Lutein and Zeaxanthin. These nutrients support brain function, improve memory, and may also help reduce the risk of cognitive decline.

Dark Chocolate: Dark chocolate with high cocoa content (70% or higher) contains flavonoids, caffeine, and antioxidants that can improve blood flow to the brain, enhance cognitive function, and boost mood. Enjoying dark chocolate in moderation can provide brain-boosting benefits.

Legumes: Beans, Lentils, Chickpeas, and Green peas are rich in fiber, protein, vitamins (like folate and B vitamins), minerals (such as iron and magnesium), and antioxidants. These nutrients support brain health, stabilize blood sugar levels, and improve cognitive function.

Incorporating a variety of these nutrient-rich foods into your diet can help fuel your brain, protect memory and thinking skills, and support overall brain health. Remember to enjoy these foods as part of a balanced diet for optimal cerebral function.

Managing Meals

Managing meals can be challenging, but there are several strategies to help streamline the process and ensure both the caregiver and the individual with dementia are adequately nourished. Here are some suggestions:

- Meal Planning: Plan meals ahead of time to reduce stress and ensure balanced nutrition. Create a weekly or monthly meal plan that includes simple, easy-to-prepare dishes.

- Preparation and Batch Cooking: Prep ingredients in advance and consider batch-cooking meals that can be portioned and frozen for later use. This saves time and ensures there are always nutritious meals available.
- Simple and Nutritious Recipes: Choose recipes that are simple to prepare with minimal ingredients and cooking steps. Focus on nutrient-dense foods like lean proteins, whole grains, fruits, and vegetables.
- Finger Foods and Easy-to-Eat Options: Offer finger foods and easy-to-eat options that require minimal utensils and can be eaten on the go. This can be especially helpful if the individual with dementia has difficulty with utensils or sitting down for a full meal.
- Routine and Structure: Establish a mealtime routine with set meal times and a designated eating area. Consistency can help reduce confusion and agitation during meal times.
- Provide Assistance and Supervision: Offer assistance and supervision during meal times as needed. This may include helping with meal preparation, setting the table, and providing verbal cues to encourage eating.
- Adaptations for Eating Challenges: Adapt to eating challenges such as swallowing difficulties or sensory issues. This may involve modifying food textures, using adaptive utensils, or providing alternative meal options.
- Encourage Independence: Encourage independence and autonomy in meal-related tasks whenever possible. Allow the individual with dementia to participate in meal preparation or decision-making to maintain a sense of dignity and control.
- Monitor Hydration: Offer fluids throughout the day to ensure adequate hydration. Encourage the individual

with dementia to drink water, juice, or other hydrating beverages regularly.

- Seek Support and Respite: Don't hesitate to seek support from other family members, friends, or community resources. Consider arranging for respite care to allow caregivers time for self-care and relaxation.

By implementing these strategies, dementia caregivers can effectively manage meals while prioritizing the nutritional needs and well-being of both themselves and the individuals they care for.

Meal Prep is an Art in Caregiving

Creating meals that are both simple and rich in sensory appeal is crucial in dementia care. Simplifying meals goes beyond minimizing ingredients or steps; it involves crafting inviting and nourishing experiences. Opt for colorful plates and diverse textures to make dining visually stimulating and engaging, turning mealtime into a feast for the eyes as well as the palate. Incorporating aromatic herbs not only adds layers of flavor but also acts as a natural appetite stimulant, making each dish more appealing. Establishing thoughtful mealtime rituals plays a pivotal role in ensuring that meals nourish both the body and the soul, transforming everyday dining into meaningful moments of connection and care.

Practical Feeding Tips

- Create a Calm Environment: Minimize distractions and create a peaceful atmosphere for meals. Turn off the TV and reduce background noise to help your loved one focus on eating.

- Serve Nutritious Meals: Offer a variety of healthy, well-balanced meals and snacks that are appealing and easy to eat. Consider foods that are familiar and comforting to your loved one, and accommodate any dietary restrictions or preferences.
- Encourage Independence: Allow your loved one to feed themselves as much as possible, even if it means providing finger foods or adaptive utensils. Offer assistance and support as needed, but avoid rushing or taking over completely.
- Provide Assistance with Dignity: If your loved one requires assistance with feeding, offer support respectfully. Use gentle prompts and cues to encourage eating, and respect their pace and preferences.
- Be Patient and Flexible: Mealtime can be challenging for individuals with dementia, so it is important to remain patient and understanding. Be prepared for changes in appetite, mood, and behavior, and be flexible in your approach to mealtime.
- Monitor Hydration: Encourage your loved one to drink plenty of fluids throughout the day to prevent dehydration. Offer beverages regularly and consider using a variety of cups or straws to make drinking easier. Non-spill travel cups are ideal.
- Watch for Signs of Discomfort: Pay attention to nonverbal cues and body language that may indicate discomfort or difficulty swallowing. Consult a healthcare professional for guidance if your loved one experiences swallowing problems or choking.
- Celebrate Successes: Acknowledge and celebrate small victories and accomplishments during mealtime, whether trying a new food or finishing a meal independently.

Positive reinforcement can help maintain motivation and enjoyment during meals.

CHEWING AND SWALLOWING DIFFICULTIES

If someone with dementia is experiencing swallowing difficulties, also known as dysphagia, it's important to take steps to ensure their safety and well-being. The same goes for difficulties with chewing; it can be challenging to ensure they are receiving proper nutrition while also preventing choking or other complications.

Pocketing or Pouching

Pouching or Pocketing is when someone puts more food in before the previous bite has been swallowed. This means keeping food in the cheeks or back of the mouth rather than swallowing fully.

Here are some actions you can take:

- Consult a Healthcare Professional: Speak to the person's healthcare provider, such as a doctor or speech therapist, to assess the severity of the swallowing problem and determine appropriate interventions.
- Modify Food and Liquid Consistency: Adjust the texture of food and liquids to make them easier to swallow. This may involve thickening liquids to reduce the risk of aspiration or providing softer, pureed foods that are easier to chew and swallow.
- Support During Meals: Offer assistance and supervision during meals to ensure the person eats and drinks safely. Encourage small, frequent meals and snacks to prevent fatigue and reduce the risk of choking.

- Positioning: Help the person sit upright during meals to facilitate swallowing and reduce the risk of aspiration. Avoid feeding them while lying down or in a reclined position.
- Monitor Swallowing: Pay close attention to the person's swallowing abilities and watch for signs of difficulty, such as coughing, choking, or pocketing food in the mouth.
- Provide Oral Care: Maintain good oral hygiene by gently brushing the person's teeth and gums after meals to prevent infections and maintain oral health, which can impact swallowing function.
- Encourage Swallowing Exercises: Work with a speech therapist to implement swallowing exercises designed to strengthen the muscles involved in swallowing and improve coordination.
- Use Adaptive Equipment: Consider using adaptive equipment, such as special utensils, cups, or feeding devices, to facilitate eating and drinking for individuals with swallowing difficulties.
- Cut Food into Small Pieces: Cut food into bite-sized pieces to make it easier to chew and swallow. This can reduce the risk of choking and make eating more manageable for the individual.
- Create a Safe Eating Environment: Minimize distractions and create a calm, supportive environment for meals to reduce anxiety and improve focus during eating.
- Document Changes and Progress: Track any changes in the person's swallowing function and report them to their healthcare provider. Documenting progress and adjustments to the swallowing management plan can help ensure ongoing care and support.

It's essential to approach swallowing difficulties in individuals with dementia with patience, compassion, and attention to their unique needs. Working closely with healthcare professionals and implementing appropriate interventions can help improve the safety and quality of life.

INVOLVEMENT IN HOUSEHOLD TASKS

Daily tasks become more important for people with mental decline. Simple chores become chances to show their abilities and maintain independence. This change turns routine activities into opportunities for them to feel accomplished and respected.

Maintaining a sense of purpose is vital for individuals living with dementia. While cognitive decline may present challenges, fostering a feeling of purpose can enhance well-being and quality of life.

Promoting a Sense of Purpose

Doing chores at home is more than physical work for those with memory impairment. Even simple tasks like folding laundry or setting the table, which might not seem important to others, become meaningful expressions of self while experiencing dementia. These activities help maintain self-esteem and a sense of belonging when they become part of daily life. This connection is vital, providing comfort and preventing feelings of isolation. By choosing tasks that reflect the person's past interests and abilities, we can help them feel valued beyond their condition.

Here are some strategies to promote a sense of purpose in dementia care:

- Engage in Meaningful Activities: Encourage participation in activities that align with the individual's interests, hobbies, and past experiences. These could include gardening, painting, music therapy, or simple household tasks. Tailor activities to the individual's current abilities and preferences to maximize engagement and satisfaction.
- Provide Opportunities for Contribution: Even in the later stages of dementia, individuals can still contribute meaningfully. Assign simple tasks that match their abilities, such as folding laundry, setting the table, or sorting objects. Acknowledge and praise their efforts to boost self-esteem and reinforce a sense of purpose.
- Emphasize Familiarity and Routine: Establishing familiar routines can provide structure and a sense of security for individuals with dementia. Engage in activities they are familiar with, such as cooking family recipes, listening to favorite songs, or reminiscing about past experiences. Consistency and predictability can help reduce anxiety and confusion.
- Encourage Social Interaction: Facilitate opportunities for socialization and connection with others. Arrange visits with family and friends, participate in group activities at a local community center or senior living facility, or join dementia-specific support groups. Meaningful social interactions can foster a sense of belonging and purpose.
- Validate Emotions and Accomplishments: Recognize and validate the individual's emotions, accomplishments, and contributions. Offer praise, encouragement, and positive reinforcement to boost self-esteem and confidence. Celebrate small victories and milestones, reinforcing their sense of worth and purpose.

- Promote Independence and Decision-Making: Empower individuals with dementia to make choices and participate in decision-making whenever possible. Offer options and respect their preferences, even if they require assistance or guidance. Encouraging autonomy fosters a sense of control and purpose.
- Explore Therapeutic Interventions: Consider incorporating therapeutic interventions that promote a sense of purpose and well-being. This could include animal-assisted therapy, reminiscence therapy, art or music therapy, or sensory stimulation activities. Tailor interventions to the individual's interests and abilities for maximum benefit.
- Provide Opportunities for Spiritual Expression: For individuals with spiritual or religious beliefs, provide opportunities for prayer, meditation, or participation in religious services or rituals. Spiritual practices can offer comfort, meaning, and a sense of connection to something greater than oneself.

By incorporating these strategies, caregivers can help individuals maintain a sense of purpose, dignity, and fulfillment throughout the disease's progression.

Streamlining Tasks for Enhanced Safety

Caring for individuals with dementia involves adapting tasks and environments to promote safety, independence, and overall well-being. Task simplification strategies focus on breaking down activities into manageable steps while prioritizing safety considerations. Here are several ways to implement task simplification and enhance safety in dementia care:

- Clear and Simple Instructions: Provide clear and concise instructions for tasks, using simple language and visual cues whenever possible. Break down complex tasks into smaller steps, and provide verbal prompts or demonstrations as needed to guide the individual through each step.
- Reduce Environmental Distractions: To help individuals focus on the task at hand and minimize distractions in the environment. Turn off the television or radio, reduce background noise, and eliminate clutter or unnecessary objects that may cause confusion or agitation.
- Use Visual Aids and Reminders: Utilize visual aids, such as written instructions, pictures, or diagrams, to supplement verbal instructions and reinforce understanding. Place visual reminders in prominent locations to cue individuals about daily routines, safety procedures, or important tasks.
- Establish Consistent Routines: Establishing consistent daily routines can provide structure and predictability for individuals with dementia. Create a daily schedule that includes regular meal times, hygiene routines, and recreational activities, and stick to the schedule as much as possible to reduce confusion and anxiety.
- Break Tasks into Manageable Steps: Break down complex tasks, such as dressing or meal preparation, into smaller, more manageable steps. Focus on one step at a time, providing guidance and support as needed, and allow the individual to complete each step at their own pace.
- Adapt the Environment for Safety: Make modifications to the home environment to enhance safety and reduce the risk of accidents or injuries. Install grab bars in bathrooms, remove tripping hazards such as rugs or loose

cords, and use childproof locks on cabinets containing hazardous items.

- Provide Supervision and Assistance: Offer supervision and assistance as needed during tasks that may pose safety risks, such as cooking, bathing, or using household appliances. Be attentive to signs of fatigue, frustration, or confusion, and step in to provide guidance or support as necessary.
- Encourage Independence and Participation: While providing support and supervision, encourage individuals to participate in tasks to the best of their ability. Offer choices and opportunities for decision-making, and praise efforts and accomplishments to boost self-esteem and confidence.
- Monitor and Adapt as Needed: Continuously monitor the individual's abilities and adjust task simplification strategies accordingly. As the disease progresses, be prepared to modify tasks, routines, and safety measures to accommodate changing needs and abilities.

By implementing task simplification strategies and prioritizing safety considerations, caregivers can create a supportive environment that promotes independence, reduces stress, and enhances the overall quality of life for individuals living with dementia.

Adapting household tasks to align with the abilities of those in decline is akin to translating a beloved book into a new language; the essence must be preserved even as the form changes. Simplification does not imply reduction but refinement, stripping tasks to their core elements to align with diminished capabilities while ensuring safety remains paramount. This might mean reimagining cooking activities to involve non-heat-related preparation or gardening with silk flowers to eliminate the risks associated with outdoor elements.

The objective here is to maintain the individual's engagement in meaningful activity while constructing a framework for maintaining safety. This delicate yet crucial balance ensures that participation in household tasks remains a source of empowerment rather than a risk of harm. In this space, the individual can confidently navigate within the boundaries of their existing abilities.

Encouraging Participation Without Pressure

The line between encouragement and coercion is fine, yet it must be navigated with the utmost sensitivity in dementia care. To invite participation is to offer a hand, not to impose a leash. It demands an attunement to the person's rhythms and moods, recognizing moments when engagement is possible and when withdrawal is necessary. This approach asks for patience, for the understanding that refusal does not equate to failure but to an assertion of self in the only way possible at the moment. Encouragement becomes a soft invitation, extended with an open hand and a willingness to accept the response, whatever it may be. In this space, where participation is devoid of pressure, the individual finds the freedom to engage on their terms, discovering within themselves the capacity to still contribute, however modestly, to the tapestry of daily life.

Recognizing and Celebrating Contributions

Acknowledging even small contributions has the power to affirm and uplift. Recognition goes beyond praise, reflecting the person's worth and abilities back onto them. It is seen in smiles, felt in warm words and simple rewards. Celebrating contributions validates the efforts of individuals with dementia, reinforcing their sense of accomplishment. This practice requires mindfulness, actively seeking and honoring the positive amidst loss. Every task completed, no matter how small, is celebrated for its effort and intention. This recognition, filled with gratitude and respect, nourishes the spirit and encourages further engagement, boosting confidence and self-esteem.

In dementia care, involvement in household tasks is more than just an activity; it is a vital connection to purpose and self-respect. By adjusting tasks for safety and simplicity and offering encouragement without pressure, caregivers create an environment where participation is meaningful. Recognizing and celebrating every contribution enriches this environment, enforcing self-esteem and preserving identity. In this setting, every action is significant, and each task is a thread in daily life that connects individuals to purpose, belonging, and self.

IMPORTANCE OF CONSISTENT DAILY ROUTINES

With dementia, carefully designed and consistently maintained daily routines offer vital stability amidst varying memory and cognitive abilities. Setting regular times for meals, medication, activities, and rest can provide structure and stability for the caregiver and the person in need. Incorporating activities they enjoy can help stimulate their mind, reduce boredom, and improve their overall mood. These activities could include listening to music, doing puzzles, gardening, or going for walks. This consistency provides essential comfort, easing anxiety and promoting peace of mind. However, it's important to incorporate flexibility into these routines to accommodate changes in capabilities and emotional states.

When adjusting routines, changes should be introduced gradually to minimize disruptions and maintain a calm environment. Striking a balance between consistency and adaptability allows you to create a supportive atmosphere tailored to unique needs. This reflects a caregiver's dedication to empathy, laying the groundwork for compassionate care.

Home Care Service

Maintaining stability amidst constantly shifting schedules can profoundly affect one's life. Recognizing when to step away and attend to personal matters is crucial. In such moments, seeking the support of home care services can provide invaluable assistance, ensuring high-quality care while giving the caregiver the necessary time and space to address their own needs and responsibilities.

Home care services allow you to regain a sense of control and feel covered when you can't always be present for your loved one. Having compassionate, professional at-home caregivers provides the relief and support you need and deserve.

Home care is personalized elderly assistance with everyday activities around the house, such as bathing, cleaning, meal prep, and medication reminders. It provides a sense of reassurance and assistance when you're unable to be with your loved one around the clock.

ADDRESSING SLEEP CHALLENGES FOR BETTER QUALITY REST

Understanding Sleep Changes

In the world of dementia, nighttime often brings restlessness instead of recuperation, with insomnia and wandering becoming very common and very frustrating for everyone involved. These disruptions can show us how the brain struggles with natural rhythms promoting recovery. Insomnia steals rest and wandering in the dark seeks familiarity. Sadly, both of these can lead to increased disorientation. Deep understanding and customized approaches are needed to restore peace at night and realign these disrupted rhythms. Sleep is absolutely imperative for our natural, nightly repair of mind and body, and arguably is equally important as adequate nutrition.

Soothing Elements

Adding calming elements to the home helps meet the sensory needs of those with dementia, creating a peaceful atmosphere. Soft lighting, soothing colors, aromatherapy diffusers, and familiar objects bring a sense of comfort and continuity, offering relief from the confusion and frustration that often come with dementia. Additionally, using textures and materials that encourage touch can provide comfort and gentle stimulation, maintaining connections to the physical world. Aromatherapy is great for helping you relax, boost your mood, improve focus, relieve stress, and help you fall asleep.

Creating a Sleep-Friendly Environment

Creating a peaceful and, more importantly, comfortable sleep environment is essential for restful nights. This space should be carefully designed to promote calmness through subdued lighting and sound, along with cozy bedding. Managing noise might mean reducing the volume or using a sound machine; it is about creating a soothing atmosphere. Light control is crucial, signaling to the brain that it is time to rest, but a dim nightlight can provide reassurance for those who wake up disoriented. Temperature also plays a role, with cooler air and warm blankets helping to relax the body. When combined effectively, these elements turn the bedroom into a welcoming sanctuary for sleep. But ultimately, a comfortable bed is imperative for the prospect of falling and staying asleep.

Establishing a Routine that Supports Sleep

The rhythm of a nightly routine gently guides individuals from the day's busyness to the night's calmness. Like a well-trodden path, this familiar sequence signals to both body and mind that it is time to rest. Whether it involves changing into their pajamas, brushing their teeth, reading a book, or listening to calming music, each step is a form of reverence, preparing one for sleep. The scent of Lavender, Jasmine, or even Sandalwood can also enhance the sense of calm. Each component of this routine should be chosen carefully, providing comfort and creating a pathway to sleep that even those with dementia can easily follow. Make sure they're getting enough daylight to help with their circadian rhythm and avoid caffeine, sugar, and alcohol, which tend to disrupt sleep. Removing electronics such as cell phones, computers, or laptops can improve sleep quality too.

When to Seek Professional Help

Sometimes, despite tender and patient efforts, dealing with sleep issues in dementia can turn from an annoyance into feeling completely overwhelmed. Especially if it becomes disruptive to the entire household. At such times, it is wise to consider seeking professional help. Healthcare providers can offer valuable interventions and understanding by looking at the whole person rather than just the symptoms. Sleep aids, when prescribed carefully, can be helpful tools, gently guiding the mind toward sleep. Collaborating with professionals allows new strategies to be woven into existing care plans, strengthening overall support. It is a brave step but shows the caregiver's commitment to supporting their loved one through both day and night. Always be mindful of these commitments, which can be extremely challenging at the moment. However, it can provide the caregiver emotional reassurance once your loved one has passed on, remembering that you explored every avenue available.

KEEPING THE HOME ENVIRONMENT SAFE

Creating a safe living space for those with dementia also involves careful planning. Every aspect, from furniture layout to appliances, needs thoughtful consideration. The environment should address the challenges of cognitive decline and anticipate changing needs. It requires foresight to identify and address potential hazards with innovation and compassion.

Identifying and Mitigating Risks

An essential first step is conducting a thorough home evaluation, examining each room for potential hazards that may not be obvious. This evaluation goes beyond surface-level dangers, considering how individuals' limiting abilities interact with their surroundings. A checklist is a valuable tool for caregivers, guiding them through a systematic assessment covering everything from slippery floors to accessible emergency exits. Improvements include securing loose rugs, leveling doorway thresholds, rearranging furniture for clear pathways, securing cords, using grab bars, and removing any other potential slips, trips, and fall hazards. This proactive approach reduces accident risks and empowers caregivers with practical strategies to enhance the safety of their loved ones.

Minimizing Clutter

Clutter can be problematic for individuals with dementia, as it adds confusion and increases the risk of accidents. Decluttering goes beyond just tidying up—it is a way to prevent falls and reduce anxiety by simplifying the environment. We create a safer and clearer space by removing unnecessary items and keeping only the essentials. This clarity helps individuals navigate their daily activities more confidently and assists in minimizing hoarding behaviors.

Use of Safety Devices

In today's tech-driven world, using technology to make environments safer for dementia patients offers hope. Thoughtfully chosen safety devices and technologies can significantly lower everyday risks. Devices like automatic shut-off switches for appliances help prevent fires, and motion sensor lights light up paths at night, providing reassurance. Though seemingly basic, these technologies are game-changers, creating a safety net that lets individuals move around more freely and securely. Integrating these devices is not just about preventing accidents; it is about preserving independence and giving people the confidence to interact with their environment.

Creating a Support Network

Various strategies are essential to creating a safe environment. As we concentrate on making the home safe, we are mindful of the wider dementia care context, where all strategies collaborate to uphold dignity and independence in addition to safety. These go beyond environmental risk mitigation, safety devices, and preparing for emergencies, to include building community support.

Building a solid support network is crucial for safety in dementia care. This network includes neighbors, friends, and local emergency services, providing a safety net beyond the home. It offers practical help and emotional support for caregivers as well as individuals with dementia. Creating this network involves reaching out to the community and uniting everyone to help ensure wellness. Each measure should help contribute to a community living space that protects well-being, showing care through foresight. This comprehensive view can act as a director, recognizing the trust given to us and our important role in someone's final stages of life.

EMERGENCY PREPAREDNESS FOR CAREGIVER'S

Preparing for emergencies is fundamental in dementia care. It means more than gathering supplies and making plans. It reinforces the caregiver's dedication to keeping their loved one safe during tough times. It should include important medical information, preferences for care, and practical details. It also lays out who will do what and how everyone will communicate during an emergency. This plan becomes a field guide for caregivers when things get chaotic.

Emergency Kits

Alongside creating the emergency plan, caregivers need to put together emergency kits. These kits contain basics like water, food, medication, weather-appropriate clothing, and things specifically for someone with dementia. If oxygen is used, ensure easy access to portable tanks. Purchase extra medication; keep other supplies well stocked. They might include comforting items, copies of important documents, and a supply of medications. Each item is chosen to be useful and comforting during uncertain times. Keeping these kits in easy-to-reach places and checking them regularly shows readiness and helps ease worries during emergencies. If you need immediate assistance in an emergency situation, dial 911. Provide copies of the person's medical history, a list of medications, doctor information, and family contacts to people other than the primary caregiver.

Communication Strategies

Good communication becomes a lifeline during emergencies, linking caregivers to their support network. Strategies vary, like setting up a communication tree to spread messages quickly or preparing cue cards for responders that explain the person's dementia-related needs. These planned approaches ensure caregivers' voices are heard, and the person with dementia gets the help they need, even in chaotic situations.

DEMENTIA CAREGIVER'S GUIDE
REVIEW REQUEST PAGE

Make a Difference with Your Review

"There will come a time when your loved one will be gone, and you will find comfort in the fact that you were their caregiver."

— KAREN COETZER

I trust that this book has already offered valuable insights. As you continue reading, I'm confident that you'll find yourself increasingly equipped and empowered for your journey as a caregiver. Your evolving confidence will serve as a steady guide, enhancing both your skills and your compassion along the way.

I'm reaching out to extend my heartfelt appreciation for your interest in my book. Your decision to explore its pages means a great deal to me, and I'm truly grateful for your support. If you could spare a moment to share your thoughts through a review, it would be an honor beyond words and serve as a tremendous source of encouragement to others on this journey. Thank you for considering this request and being a part of this meaningful exchange.

Your review might just be a beacon for others...

navigating the challenges of caregiving.

looking for a trusted resource.

seeking guidance and support.

Simply scan the QR code below to leave your review.

Thank you from the bottom of my heart.

Warmest,

Shea Wolfe

PS - Bringing value to others is the true essence of living a meaningful life. When we dedicate ourselves to making a positive impact, we not only enrich the lives of those around us but also find fulfillment and purpose in our own journey. In a world where kindness and compassion are often the most precious gifts we can give, let us strive to be a beacon of light, inspiring others and spreading warmth wherever we go.

CHAPTER 5

NAVIGATING THE HEALTHCARE SYSTEM

This chapter is about building a care team, working with a care manager, and handling specialist care for dementia. It emphasizes teamwork, clear communication, and making informed choices in the healthcare system. By doing this, caregivers can create a thorough care plan that adapts to the person's changing needs. With a strong team, you will be able to navigate the challenges of dementia care more effectively. Working with healthcare professionals in dementia care is like having skilled navigators help to guide you through rough seas. Their expertise helps them make informed decisions at every step, ensuring thorough and flexible care that meets the individual's needs.

BUILDING A CARE TEAM

Assembling a care team where each member brings unique skills to create a complete picture. This team might include doctors, nurses, and occupational therapists, working together to tailor care strategies. It is important to choose professionals who collaborate well and value input from caregivers. Each will bring a critical layer of expertise to manage health complexities. Social workers, legal advisors, and care managers offer guidance in navigating the labyrinth of dementia care logistics and legalities. The task demands a keen eye for strengths and the limitations of potential contributions.

This might be a family member taking on daily care tasks, a friend managing appointments and outings, and a professional caregiver stepping in for specialized health needs. Effective team collaboration relies on clear, consistent, and open communication. Scheduled meetings, whether in person or online, allow for real-time updates and exchanges. Caregivers play a crucial role in bridging gaps between professionals and keeping the care recipient's needs in focus.

One helpful step is to create a care dossier, which includes medical history, medications, and observed behaviors. This dossier is continuously updated when new evidence and information become available. Sharing this document with the team ensures everyone is informed and can make cohesive care recommendations.

When opinions differ, care providers can help find common ground by focusing on shared goals and using the care dossier to guide discussions. This approach makes communication smoother and strengthens the caregiver's role as an advocate in care decisions.

Role of Care Manager

Navigating the healthcare system can be overwhelming. That is where a care manager comes in. They are like guides, helping you understand medical appointments, treatment choices, and care services. They handle the details so you can concentrate on providing care. To find the right care manager, interview a few candidates. Make sure they have experience specifically with dementia care and share your teamwork approach. This helps set you up for a helpful partnership.

Navigating Specialist Care

The journey through dementia often necessitates the involvement of specialists and professionals who bring deep expertise in specific aspects of dementia care and pre-existing conditions. However, securing appointments with such experts can be complex, marked by long waiting lists and the challenge of preparing for meaningful and productive consultations.

The care manager can facilitate preparation for these appointments by prioritizing questions and concerns and ensuring that the most pressing issues are addressed. Additionally, caregivers can record observations and questions in the care dossier, providing specialists with a detailed picture of the individual's current condition and enhancing the efficacy of consultations.

MEDICATION MANAGEMENT AND SAFETY

Handling medications is a cornerstone of ensuring safety and promoting well-being in dementia care. Caregivers are responsible for meticulously managing each medication, comprehending their mechanisms of action, and discerning how they interact with one another. This process entails deciphering prescriptions precisely and maintaining vigilant observation for potential side effects. By doing so, caregivers can ensure that medications contribute positively to the health and comfort of those under their care rather than posing risks.

The complexity of managing medications in dementia care necessitates a systematic approach. Caregivers must administer medications as prescribed and monitor their effects closely. This involves documenting any observed changes in behavior, cognitive function, or physical health. Keeping a detailed journal serves as an invaluable tool in this regard. The journal should include comprehensive information such as the medications' names and dosages, the administration's timing, and any observed reactions or changes in symptoms.

Your regular communication with healthcare professionals is not just important; it's essential for effective medication management in dementia care. By updating healthcare providers about any observed changes in the individual's condition or response to medications, you are playing a crucial role in the care process. Additionally, seeking guidance on managing medication-related challenges, such as addressing side effects or adjusting dosages, is a testament to your dedication and commitment to the well-being of the individual under your care.

Understanding Prescriptions

The first step is to understand the prescriptions from healthcare providers very clearly. Each medication's dosage and timing are crucial for the individual's well-being. This means learning about each medication's names, doses, purposes, benefits, and possible side effects. Talking openly with doctors and pharmacists helps caregivers gain this understanding, turning confusing medical terms into useful information they can act on.

Organizing and Administering Medications

Once you understand why each medication is prescribed, the next step is to focus on organizing and administering them safely and consistently. This involves using pill organizers as more than containers—they become visual reminders of daily tasks. Keeping medication logs and detailed records helps track when and how each dose is taken, adding accountability and creating a clear history of care. These tools, though simple, are essential for maintaining a routine that reduces risks and ensures medications work as intended.

Moreover, your efforts to promote medication adherence can significantly impact treatment outcomes. You, as a caregiver, play a vital role in supporting individuals with dementia in adhering to their prescribed medication schedules. Your proactive approach can make a real difference in the individual's health and well-being.

Monitoring for Side Effects

As medications become part of the daily routine, it is crucial to watch closely for any changes they might cause in the individual's health and behavior. Side effects, even from seemingly harmless medications, must be identified and addressed quickly. This means more than just casual observation—it involves carefully noting and analyzing any changes in mood, thinking, or physical health. Caregivers must act as vigilant guards, alert to any signs of trouble, and be ready to discuss concerns with healthcare providers. Taking this proactive approach ensures that medications are helping and providing support without adding more problems.

Collaboration with Pharmacists

Pharmacists are key partners in ensuring medication safety and effectiveness. They offer valuable advice on things like when to take medication and how to manage side effects. By working closely with pharmacists, caregivers can tap into the professional expertise and better manage the complex medication routines of dementia care. This collaboration, enhanced by knowledge, organization, and vigilance, ensures medications are used safely to improve the lives of those with dementia.

In addition to pharmacological interventions, caregivers should explore complementary approaches to enhance overall well-being. These may include non-pharmacological interventions such as cognitive stimulation activities, physical exercise, social engagement, and nutritional support. Integrating these holistic approaches into the care plan can complement medication management efforts and contribute to a comprehensive approach to dementia care.

In conclusion, effective medication management is paramount in dementia care, requiring careful attention, documentation, and collaboration with healthcare professionals. By adopting a proactive and holistic approach, caregivers can optimize treatment outcomes and enhance the quality of life for individuals with dementia.

RECOGNIZING AND ADDRESSING PAIN

Pain often goes unspoken in the realm of mental decline. Caregivers must learn to recognize subtle signs, like facial expressions or changes in behavior, that indicate discomfort. Observing physical changes can also reveal hidden pain.

Caregivers must be especially vigilant at interpreting these cues and advocating for their loved one's needs, even when verbal communication fails.

Identifying Signs of Pain

Nonverbal and verbal signs of pain can include limping, grimacing, restlessness, constant twitching, rubbing a body part, tensing up, pacing, moving, or unwillingness to sit down, moaning, crying, sighing, and even heavy breathing.

Pain Management Strategies

Managing pain in dementia care requires a balanced approach that combines medicine with compassionate alternatives. Medications should be used carefully, always considering potential side effects. Alongside pharmaceuticals, physical therapy, massage, acupuncture, and topical creams can relieve pain. Each approach should be chosen based on the individual's needs and preferences, with input from healthcare professionals to ensure a tailored plan that respects the complexities of dementia.

Importance of Routine Assessments

Regular pain assessments are crucial in dementia care because both conditions are constantly changing. By using tools like adapted pain scales or keeping detailed pain diaries, caregivers can track discomfort accurately. This ongoing process of assessment and adjustment ensures that pain management strategies adapt to the individual's changing needs, ensuring effective care.

Advocating for Pain Management

Caregivers play a crucial role in advocating for pain management for individuals with dementia. They use their deep understanding of the person's needs to speak up confidently in discussions with healthcare providers. By documenting signs of pain and how the recipient responds to current treatments, caregivers provide evidence to guide decisions. In this way, caregivers emerge as advocates for addressing pain, ensuring that the individual's needs are not only acknowledged but promptly addressed.

REGULAR HEALTH SCREENINGS AND CHECK-UPS

Regular health check-ups and evaluations are essential for early detection and intervention of dementia care. These scheduled appointments act as vital checkpoints to identify potential health issues before they escalate into more serious complications. This proactive approach not only enhances the individual's quality of life but also mitigates the risk of exacerbating underlying health conditions.

Moreover, these appointments offer invaluable comprehensive assessment and holistic care planning opportunities. Beyond the primary focus on cognitive function, these evaluations encompass a broad spectrum of health domains, including physical, emotional, and social well-being. Through a collaborative effort involving healthcare providers, caregivers, and the individual, these assessments can yield valuable insights into the holistic needs of the person living with dementia.

Additionally, regular health check-ups foster a culture of continuous monitoring and adjustment in the management of dementia care. They provide a platform for ongoing dialogue and partnership between caregivers and healthcare professionals, facilitating the exchange of information, concerns, and goals related to the individual's health and care. This collaborative approach enables tailored interventions and personalized care plans to be developed, ensuring that the individual's evolving needs are met with precision and compassion.

Scheduling and Planning

Planning these evaluations requires careful consideration of the individual's abilities and the practical aspects of caregiving. This involves creating a calendar that includes upcoming screenings and past evaluations and managing appointment logistics. Digital reminders are helpful in ensuring caregivers do not miss appointments, serving as active aids in the process. Transportation and support arrangements are also crucial for safeguarding a smooth journey to each appointment.

Preventive Care Focus

Regular health screenings and evaluations prioritize prevention, recognizing that addressing small changes early can prevent larger problems later. These assessments cover various aspects of health, including cardiovascular health and cognitive function, each playing a vital role in overall well-being. They also emphasize the importance of vaccinations, vision, and hearing checks, and evaluations for other health conditions that can impact dementia. This holistic approach views individuals as more than their diagnosis, focusing on their unique needs and strengths. Plan appointments around the person's daily routine and schedule them when they are most alert. They also group appointments together to make things easier. Communication tools help keep all healthcare providers informed, making sure everyone is on the same page.

Documenting Health Changes

Recording details of health changes, treatment responses, and new symptoms, often in diaries, charts, or digital formats, adds to the health dossier and helps healthcare providers understand the individual's experiences beyond clinical settings. Sharing these records during appointments ensures that care decisions are well-informed and personalized. This proactive approach, combining strategic scheduling and thorough documentation, creates a strong foundation for managing healthcare in dementia. It respects the individual's history and current needs, guiding their journey with thoughtful care and foresight.

Improving Dementia Care

The landscape of healthcare policies and priorities has undergone significant changes, ushering in initiatives such as the annual wellness visit, which now mandates the identification of any cognitive impairment among Medicare beneficiaries. Evolving healthcare agendas and research findings have underscored the potential benefits of routine dementia screening, outweighing concerns over potential drawbacks. This paradigm shift has reshaped our approach to screening for cognitive decline, highlighting its pivotal role in older adults' healthcare, particularly as a harbinger of impending or existing dementia.

The quest for therapeutic interventions capable of delaying dementia progression has emerged as a central scientific endeavor. Numerous studies spanning decades have revealed a concerning trend: many individuals living with dementia have never received a formal diagnosis. In light of this, we must take proactive steps as family members to help identify changes in our loved ones.

MANAGING COEXISTING HEALTH CONDITIONS

In dementia care, additional health issues introduce a layer of complexity that demands meticulous attention and strategic management. Conditions such as heart disease, diabetes, arthritis, and others not only coexist with dementia but also interact with it in intricate ways, influencing the development and progression of symptoms. Rather than treating each condition separately, caregivers must adopt a holistic perspective that views the individual's health as interconnected and interdependent.

Impact of Coexisting Conditions

This holistic approach acknowledges the intricate interplay between dementia and coexisting health conditions. For instance, individuals with dementia may experience challenges in adhering to medication regimens for conditions like diabetes or hypertension, which can exacerbate both cognitive and physical symptoms. Similarly, the cognitive impairments associated with dementia may impact an individual's ability to manage their diet and lifestyle factors, further complicating the management of chronic conditions.

Furthermore, the presence of coexisting health conditions can significantly influence the trajectory of dementia and vice versa. For example, research suggests that individuals with cardiovascular risk factors, such as hypertension or high cholesterol, may be at an increased risk of developing vascular dementia due to compromised blood flow to the brain. Similarly, uncontrolled diabetes can exacerbate cognitive decline and increase the risk of dementia-related complications.

In light of these complex interactions, caregivers must adopt a comprehensive and integrated approach to managing coexisting health conditions in dementia care. This involves collaboration with healthcare professionals from various disciplines, including primary care physicians, neurologists, geriatricians, and specialists in the management of specific health conditions. Through multidisciplinary teamwork, caregivers can develop tailored care plans that address each individual's unique needs and challenges.

Integrated Care Approach

In light of these complex interactions, caregivers must adopt a comprehensive and integrated approach to managing coexisting health conditions in dementia care. This means sharing information and making decisions as a team, considering all aspects of the individual's health. It prioritizes managing multiple conditions simultaneously rather than one after the other. This ensures that treatments for other health issues are pursued with the same attention as the issues for dementia and are coordinated to avoid conflicts. For example, this could involve adjusting medications to prevent negative interactions or tailoring diet advice to address cognitive health and conditions like high blood pressure.

Supporting Overall Wellbeing

Managing coexisting health conditions alongside dementia requires a holistic approach focused on the individual's overall welfare. This means supporting not just physical health but also emotional and social needs often overlooked in medical care. Strategies can include engaging in activities for both physical and mental stimulation, maintaining social connections, and addressing mental health concerns like depression and anxiety. The goal is to improve quality of life, ensuring each day brings moments of joy and fulfillment.

INNOVATIONS IN DEMENTIA CARE AND TREATMENT

Emerging Therapies

New therapies are offering hope for better dementia care. Biogenetic treatments target the disease's core processes to stop cognitive decline early, while neuroplasticity-based therapies aim to restore lost functions by harnessing the brain's ability to adapt and regenerate. Though they are still being researched and tested, these innovative approaches are fueled by both science and compassion. They promise to transform how we care for those with dementia through creative breakthroughs.

Technology in Dementia Care

Parallel to the strides made in therapeutic innovation, technology has emerged as a formidable ally in dementia care, reshaping the landscape with tools and devices that enhance the quality of life, facilitate care, and promote independence. Wearable technology, for instance, offers a discreet yet powerful means of tracking as well as monitoring vital signs, detecting falls, and predicting potential health issues before they become emergencies. These devices, often seamlessly integrated into the every day, provide a continuous stream of data that can inform care decisions and interventions, ensuring responsiveness that was once the sole burden of vigilant observation. Beyond wearables, smart home technologies have transformed living spaces into environments that actively support the needs of those with dementia. Automated lighting, voice-activated devices, and GPS-enabled locators exemplify how the home can become a nurturing, safe space that accommodates the shifting realities of cognitive decline.

Participating in Clinical Trials

Deciding to join clinical trials is hopeful and practical for caregivers and those they care for. It is a step taken to seek potential benefits and contribute to understanding and treating dementia better. Finding the right trial involves careful consideration and bravery, weighing the promise of new treatments against the uncertainties of research. It starts with exploring available trials, using registries and databases that list studies based on factors like location, type of dementia, and treatment focus. This exploration, guided by healthcare professionals and supported by dementia research organizations, leads to a decision that reflects a deep commitment to pushing the boundaries of dementia care. Participating in these trials is not just about personal benefit but about believing in the collective effort to find better solutions for everyone affected by dementia.

CHAPTER 6

YOUR NEEDS AS A CAREGIVER MATTER TOO

A caregiver's day starts in the soft glow of dawn—a routine filled with tasks and emotions. While their dedication shines through, there is also the strain of stress and burnout. It is important for caregivers to acknowledge and manage this strain in order to keep providing quality care. Making sure to take care of themselves ensures they can continue caring for their loved ones throughout the challenges of dementia care.

UNDERSTANDING CAREGIVER STRESS AND BURNOUT

Groundhog Day

When your days feel the same, it often indicates a sense of monotony in your daily life. You may find yourself going through similar activities, tasks, or experiences day after day, without much variation or excitement. This feeling can result in a sense of boredom, frustration, or even disconnection from the passage of time.

Changing things up and making caregiving interesting for the caregiver and the person with dementia can breathe new life into the daily routine. Here are some ideas:

- Variety in Activities: Incorporate a variety of activities into the daily routine, such as arts and crafts, puzzles, music therapy, gentle exercises, gardening, or sensory stimulation activities. Rotate activities regularly to keep things fresh and engaging.
- Outdoor Time: Spend time outdoors together, whether going for a walk in nature, sitting in the garden, or enjoying a picnic. Fresh air and sunshine can lift spirits and provide a change of scenery.
- Multi-Sensory Experiences: Create multi-sensory experiences by incorporating different textures, scents, sounds, and tastes into activities. For example, you could have a sensory box filled with items of various textures to explore.
- Reminiscence Therapy: People can engage in reminiscence therapy by looking through old photos, listening to music from their youth, or talking about past experiences and memories. Reminiscing can evoke positive emotions and stimulate memories.
- Social Interaction: Arrange visits or virtual calls with friends, family members, or other residents in the assisted living home. Social interaction can provide stimulation and a sense of connection.
- Intergenerational Activities: Organize intergenerational activities with children or youth, such as reading

together, playing games, or doing simple crafts. These interactions can be mutually beneficial and bring joy to both parties.

- Themed Days or Events: Plan themed days or events based on holidays, seasons, or personal interests. For example, you could have a "beach day" with beach-themed activities and decorations or a "movie night" with popcorn and a favorite film.
- Cooking or Baking Together: Involve the person with dementia in simple cooking or baking activities, such as making cookies or preparing a favorite recipe together. Cooking can engage the senses and provide a sense of accomplishment.
- Virtual Tours or Cultural Experiences: Take virtual tours of museums, landmarks, or cultural sites from around the world. Many museums and organizations offer online tours and programs that can be enjoyed from the comfort of home.
- Adapted Games and Activities: Explore adapted versions of games and activities that are suitable for individuals with dementia, such as modified card games, trivia quizzes, or gentle exercises.

By introducing variety, creativity, and personalized experiences into the caregiving routine, you can make each day feel unique and meaningful for you and the person with dementia.

Identifying Signs of Stress and Burnout

Caregivers may not notice the subtle strain creeping in quietly amid their daily routines. Physical signs like headaches, fatigue, or weight changes hint at the body's struggle to cope. Emotionally, they might feel irritable, sad, or detached. It is important for caregivers to pause and reflect on these signs, realizing they need care too.

Caregiver stress stems from various sources, each with its own impact. The nonstop demands of caregiving can often leave little time for rest or personal activities. Financial pressures, like covering medical costs or making home modifications, add to the strain. However, the emotional toll—seeing a loved one decline, dealing with difficult behaviors, or managing family relationships—is the most burdensome aspect. Recognizing these factors helps caregivers find ways to cope and get support.

The Impact on Care

Caregiver stress can affect the quality of care given. When you feel tired, irritable, or overwhelmed, providing care with patience and attention may become more difficult. This is when you lose patience and may snap at others with a hateful tone. Don't feel guilty; this happens to everyone. It's not a sign of failure but rather a reminder that caring for oneself is equally important as caring for someone else. Often understated, forgiving oneself for circumstances out of one's control can become imperative.

Implementing one's own checklist for symptoms can help caregivers assess their well-being and prompt them to acknowledge and take action.

- Difficulty falling asleep.
- Waking up in the middle of the night.
- Getting sick more often.
- Develop chronic health problems, such as headaches, backaches, etc.
- Become upset or angry easily.
- Feeling hopeless.

Preventing Burnout

Preventing burnout is highly important. Setting realistic expectations, seeking support from groups, family, or friends, and not forgetting home care services can help provide stability. Taking care of yourself with relaxation or joyful activities can be a lifeline, helping to maintain hopefulness and resilience. Journaling can also help caregivers reflect on their experiences and coping strategies, encouraging self-awareness.

As each day starts, your own wellness becomes a central part of dementia care. Recognizing, understanding, and preventing burnout are acts of strength, ensuring they can keep going with love and endurance. The journey requires self-awareness and self-care to remain steady and guide themselves and those they care for through the difficult challenges ahead.

BALANCING WORK, LIFE, AND CAREGIVING

The delicate balance between work commitments, personal life, and caregiving responsibilities presents a formidable challenge for many individuals. Whether caring for an aging parent, a child with special needs, or a family member with a chronic illness, the juggling act of fulfilling professional obligations while attending to the needs of loved ones can be overwhelming. It cannot be stated enough that careful planning, effective time management, and a supportive network maintain one's own well-being while ensuring the quality of care provided to those who depend on them.

Finding a way through this balancing act involves working closely with employers to arrange flexible work arrangements. These arrangements could include working from home, adjusting hours, or taking on part-time roles. It is important for caregivers to communicate effectively with their employers, highlighting the value they bring while also explaining why these adjustments are necessary. By presenting a clear proposal outlining potential schedules and how communication and tasks will be managed, caregivers can show their dedication to their job and to caregiving duties. This can make it easier to discuss any potential disruptions with their employers.

Resources and Programs

The National Family Caregiver Support Program (NFCSP) provides grants to states and territories to fund various supports that help family and informal caregivers care for older adults in their homes for as long as possible.

Established in 2000, the NFCSP allocates grants to states and territories proportionate to their elderly population, aiding family and informal caregivers in providing home-based care for their loved ones. This program, authorized under Section 371 of the Older Americans Act of 1965 (Title IIIE), encompasses various supports to facilitate caregiving at home for as long as feasible.

NFCSP grantees provide five types of services:

- Information to caregivers about available services.
- Assistance to caregivers in gaining access to the services.
- Individual counseling, organization of support groups, and caregiver training.
- Respite care and supplemental services on a limited basis.

The 2016 Reauthorization of the Older Americans Act, the following specific populations of caregivers are eligible to receive services:

- Adult family members or other informal caregivers age 18 and older provide care to individuals 60 years of age and older.
- Adult family members or other informal caregivers age 18 and older provide care to individuals of any age with Alzheimer's disease and related disorders.
- Older relatives (not parents) age 55 and older provide care to children under the age of 18.
- Older relatives, including parents, age 55 and older, provide care to adults ages 18-59 with disabilities.

Family caregivers express their individual needs and preferences for the specific programs and services they require at different stages. Moreover, the availability of programs and services varies across states and communities. Thankfully, numerous national organizations and initiatives exist to offer guidance and support for developing and enhancing programs.

Other resources include:

- Eldercare Locator.
- Family Caregiver Alliance-National Center on Caregiving.
- Caregiver Action Network - caregiveraction.org
- AARP Family Caregiving.
- Community Resource Finder - communityresourcefinder.org
- Alzheimer's Association - alz.org
- Administration for Community Living: Inventory of Federal Caregiver Programs & Initiatives.

The Power of Positivity

Within the whirlwind of caregiving duties, maintaining a positive mindset serves as a guiding light, helping nurturers navigate challenges with persistence and optimism. This positivity is not about ignoring the tough parts of caregiving but choosing to focus on its rewards—the deep connections formed by personal growth and the satisfaction of providing comfort. Practicing gratitude is key, acknowledging small victories and moments of joy each day. This practice becomes a source of strength, countering stress and fatigue, and giving care providers a sense of purpose and fulfillment in their daily lives.

LEVERAGING FMLA FOR FAMILY SUPPORT

The Family and Medical Leave Act (FMLA) is a federal law in the United States that provides eligible employees up to 12 weeks of unpaid (you should be able to use any sick or annual leave if permitted}, job-protected leave per year for specific family and medical reasons. FMLA allows employees to take time off from work to care for their own serious health condition, to care for a family member with a serious health condition, or to bond with a new child (birth, adoption, or foster care). Additionally, FMLA provides for certain circumstances related to military family leave.

FMLA can be a valuable resource for individuals caring for a loved one because it allows them to take time off from work without risking their job security. This can provide the necessary flexibility for caregivers to attend to the needs of their family members without the added stress of worrying about their employment status. Whether it's accompanying a family member to medical appointments, providing hands-on care during recovery from an illness or surgery, or offering emotional support during challenging times, FMLA ensures that caregivers have the opportunity to prioritize their family responsibilities without facing negative consequences at work.

It's important to note that FMLA eligibility criteria apply, including requirements related to the size of the employer, length of employment, and the number of hours worked. Additionally, FMLA leave is unpaid, although some employers may offer paid leave options or allow employees to use accrued paid time off (such as sick leave or vacation time) during FMLA leave. Overall, FMLA serves as a vital protection for caregivers, enabling them to fulfill their caregiving responsibilities while maintaining their employment status.

FINDING AND USING RESPITE CARE SERVICES

Respite services are like a peaceful retreat for caregivers, giving them a break from their nonstop duties. It is not just about finding someone to take over difficult tasks; it is about recognizing the need for rest and personal time away from their responsibilities. Respite care is important because it acknowledges that nurturing, while fulfilling, can take a toll on a care provider's overall health.

Types of Respite Care

Respite care offers diverse options designed to meet the specific needs of caregivers and their loved ones with dementia. Unlike home care services, which cater to individuals requiring assistance with activities such as bathing, respite care primarily focuses on providing support and relief to the primary caregiver.

- In-home services offer care within the familiar surroundings of the person with dementia's home, providing continuity and minimal disruption to their routine.

- Adult daycare centers provide engaging activities and socialization opportunities for care recipients during the day, giving caregivers a break.
- Short-term residential care offers longer breaks, with individuals staying overnight or for a few days in facilities equipped to meet their needs.

Each option supports caregivers in different situations, demonstrating the flexibility and adaptability of respite care.

Accessing Respite Care

To access respite care, begin by researching available services through trusted sources like local health departments and support groups. Understanding funding options, including government programs, Medicare insurance benefits, and grants from non-profit organizations is key. Applying for these funds, though sometimes challenging, is essential for securing support and investing in the caregiver's wellness and the quality of care for their loved one. Support networks often provide guidance and practical solutions along the way. A helpful tip is to become a respite care provider yourself for your loved one and receive payment through Medicare. However, having supportive family members to assist when you need a break is also beneficial.

The Emotional Benefits of Respite Care

The emotional toll of the caregiver's role can sometimes become overwhelming. Respite care offers a break from these demands, allowing for much-needed emotional recharge. It is not only about physical rest; it is a chance for you to reconnect with yourself beyond your giving role. After a break, caregivers can return with renewed patience, empathy, and energy.

Respite care services are valuable allies in the care-providing journey, which is full of challenges and growth. They provide a practical solution for continuing care and acknowledge a caregiver's right to rest and self-nurturing. This ensures that despite the challenges, the journey also includes moments of reflection, grace, and well-deserved relaxation.

THE CAREGIVER'S FINANCES

Carefully managing financial resources is critical in caregiving. It forms the foundation of care now and in the future, helping to weather unpredictable costs. This planning is not just about numbers—it is a thoughtful effort to protect the welfare of both caregiver and care recipient. It involves creating a safety net that covers everything from medical expenses to making living spaces more comfortable and secure.

Out-of-Pocket Expenses

Caring for someone may lead to out-of-pocket expenses, which can greatly affect their long-term financial stability. To help cover expenses not covered by insurance, caregivers should explore all available financial resources, including government assistance programs. Additionally, it's crucial for caregivers to recognize their own limitations and seek outside support when needed. For assistance, refer to the resources and programs listed above.

Unlocking Financial Support for Caregivers

Discovering a wealth of resources to alleviate financial burdens for caregivers. Government programs offer subsidies and tax benefits to mitigate caregiving costs. Insurance coverage extends beyond medical expenses to include home support and necessary modifications. Local community resources provide additional assistance, such as equipment lending and discounted respite care.

Many people benefit from being at home during the early stages of dementia. Medicare will pay for up to 35 hours a week of home health care for people certified as "homebound." Medicaid will pay for in-home care if, without that in-home care, the person would require care in a nursing home.

For Medicaid compensation as a family caregiver, participation in self-direction programs, also known as Consumer Direction or Participant Direction, is typically required. These programs empower individuals needing long-term care services to have greater control over their care.

In addition to the Medicaid options listed above, non-Medicaid state programs pay relatives to provide care for a loved one with dementia. Like many Medicaid programs, these programs allow individuals who require care to choose the caregiver they see fit to provide the care. Unfortunately, not all states offer these types of programs, and they can be difficult to find.

Some long-term care insurance policies allow family members to get paid as caregivers. Contact your insurance agent and ask for a written confirmation of benefits.

Tax Benefits for the Caregiver

Certain federal tax credits and deductions may be available to caregivers. The IRS allows individuals who meet specified criteria to be claimed as dependents on federal tax returns.

Some out-of-pocket caregiving expenses may also be deductible— for example, unreimbursed medical expenses and a portion of other expenses not covered by insurance. A tax advisor can assist you in understanding the criteria for these deductions.

HANDLING FAMILY DYNAMICS AND CONFLICTS

Addressing Family Disagreements

In the intricate network of dementia caregiving at home, where each family member is like a star shining with its own light, disagreements often arise. these can cast shadows that can obscure the path to unified care. Navigating these differences relies on effective communication, where listening is just as important as speaking. To bridge the gaps of disagreement, it is essential first to understand one another's perspectives and acknowledge all concerns and emotions without immediate judgment. This empathetic approach sets the stage for productive discussions, shifting the focus from disagreement to collaboration, from individual viewpoints to shared goals. Creating a "family agreement," a written consensus on caregiving roles and responsibilities, can formalize this shift, turning verbal agreements into a concrete plan for working together.

The Role of Family Meetings

Regular family meetings, provide a space where voices come together, blending individual concerns into a shared story. These gatherings, organized and welcoming, can offer a platform to share updates on the care recipient's condition, discuss decisions, and reinforce support. Clear agendas are distributed beforehand, and an inclusive atmosphere encourages each member to contribute. Shared respect should guide the discussions, preserving dignity even when opinions differ. Like a trusted friend or a professional mediator, a neutral facilitator can help keep the meetings focused on their purpose, navigating emotional currents to reach a consensus to take positive actions.

Managing Expectations

The intricacies of family dynamics, woven with history and emotional ties, often result in varied expectations regarding caregiving roles along the care-providing journey. Aligning these expectations with the realities of dementia care requires careful calibration, balancing hopes and assumptions with the real-world challenges involved. This should invite open discussions about each family member's capabilities and limitations in caregiving and a realistic assessment of what can be achieved. Education is key in this process, providing knowledge about dementia's progression and care needs to create a shared understanding. By aligning expectations, family members can approach caregiving with empathy and build collective resilience to support the dementia care journey.

Seeking Mediation

When family disagreements escalate and threaten the stability of caregiving, seeking external mediation can offer a path to resolution. Mediation brings in a neutral third party skilled in navigating emotional conflicts. They guide discussions to uncover underlying issues and help family members find common ground. Though challenging, this process can turn conflict into cooperation, with a focus on the well-being of the person suffering from decline. Choosing a mediator experienced in dementia care issues can enhance understanding and respect. Navigating family dynamics and conflicts in caregiving requires courage and compassion. Strategies like open communication, regular family meetings, aligning expectations, and seeking mediation can help nurturers manage disagreements and maintain family support during demanding times.

CHAPTER 7

PREPARING FOR TOMORROW

The initiation of this dialogue, often marked by hesitation, unfolds under the shadow of dementia's progression. Yet this progression lends urgency to the discussions, a reminder that clarity today can prevent ambiguity tomorrow. Therefore, the timing of these talks is strategic, rooted in the present, yet deeply aware of the inevitable. We must embrace the emotional and spiritual aspects of our loved ones' final journey.

DISCUSSING AND DOCUMENTING CARE WISHES

Encouraging caregivers and their loved ones to discuss and document care preferences involves a thorough exploration of various options. This includes considering the familiarity of home care, as well as the structured support available in residential care facilities. Decisions about treatment choices in advanced stages, including those regarding life-sustaining measures, are also critical. These considerations require a holistic perspective, taking into account the individual's physical and spiritual needs. Though challenging, this process is essential for creating a proposal that aligns with the person's beliefs.

In guiding these discussions, caregivers are prompted to contemplate not only the practical aspects of care but also the essence of the person being cared for. This ensures that the resulting care plan is not solely based on medical requirements but also reflects a loved one's identity. Caregivers must try to honor and uphold their loved one's documented care wishes. They must advocate for these preferences, even in difficult situations, to protect the person's dignity and honor their right to determine their care. But there might come a time when you can no longer care for their needs and you need help.

PLANNING FOR END-OF-LIFE

In the later stages of dementia, when memories slip away, and the person we once knew fades, care shifts towards comfort and peace, easing pain and discomfort, reducing stress, and helping them have the highest quality of life possible. For the person with dementia, the experience may be marked by a gradual fading of self-awareness, memories slipping like grains of sand through their fingers. It's a time when patience and compassion become paramount, offering comfort in the face of confusion and fear. Caregivers bear a weighty burden, straddling the line between ensuring comfort and preserving dignity, often wrestling with feelings of grief long before their loved one's physical departure. Family members and friends witness the gradual departure of the person they once knew, grieving each loss of recognition and connection, yet finding solace in moments of clarity and shared memories. In these final chapters, love and understanding become the guiding lights, illuminating the path toward acceptance and peace for all involved.

End-of-life care is a type of palliative care often covered by hospice services. Patients eligible for hospice services receive coverage of medications, durable medical equipment, medical supplies, limited home health coverage, and frequent nursing visits. Under hospice, care is focused on comfort, relieving active symptoms, and improving quality of life.

Options for Long-Term Care

Specialized Facilities

Many dementia patients eventually require care in specialized facilities such as nursing homes, assisted living facilities, or memory care units within senior living communities. These facilities are equipped to provide tailored care for individuals with dementia, including assistance with activities of daily living (ADLs), safety measures for preventing accidents and wandering off, and structured programs to engage and stimulate cognitive function.

Person-Centered Care

Effective long-term care for dementia patients emphasizes a person-centered approach, recognizing each individual's unique needs and abilities. Care plans are tailored to accommodate the individual's strengths and limitations, promoting a sense of purpose.

24/7 Supervision and Support

Dementia patients often require round-the-clock supervision and support due to safety concerns and fluctuations in cognition and behavior. Caregivers in long-term care facilities are trained to address the diverse needs of dementia patients, including assistance with medication management, meal preparation, hygiene, and mobility.

Palliative Care

Often thought of as just end-of-life care, this approach can begin at the onset of diagnosis and continue throughout treatment. It is a time to discuss what is important to you, how and where you want to be cared for, and what level of care you would want in the future. As the illness progresses, palliative care can help your family as they plan to care for you either at home, in an assisted living facility, or in a nursing home. Treatment is tailored to meet the patient's and their family's needs, taking a comprehensive approach to care. This may involve adjustments in medications to enhance comfort, behavioral health therapies to manage anxiety or depression, nutritional interventions to address dietary concerns, social services to bolster home support, and chaplain services to tackle existential matters and grief.

Hospice Care

When the time is right, usually when the prognosis is 6 months or less, the patient's neurologist or primary care physician may recommend hospice care, which focuses on comfort rather than cure. Hospice provides pain management, emotional support, and spiritual care within the familiar embrace of a home or a specialized facility. This tender and comprehensive care acknowledges the inevitability of the disease's trajectory, offering relief in the face of decline.

Embracing the Journey

Navigating end-of-life care for someone with dementia is a profound journey, filled with emotional complexity for the individual, caregivers, family, and friends alike. For the person with dementia, the experience may be marked by a gradual fading of self-awareness, memories slipping like grains of sand through their fingers. It's a time when patience and compassion become paramount, offering comfort in the face of confusion and fear. Caregivers bear a weighty burden, straddling the line between ensuring comfort and preserving dignity, often wrestling with feelings of grief long before their loved one's physical departure. Family members and friends witness the gradual departure of the person they once knew, grieving each loss of recognition and connection, yet finding solace in moments of clarity and shared memories. In these final chapters, love and understanding become the guiding lights, illuminating the path toward acceptance and peace for all involved.

FINANCIAL PLANNING AND PROTECTION

Creating a financial plan tailored to the complex needs of dementia requires a comprehensive strategy. This plan addresses a range of expenses, from immediate medical care to long-term residential needs, providing a secure financial foundation for the person with dementia.

Exploring Government Benefits

Social Security, Medicare, and Medicaid can help ease the financial burden of caregiving. Understanding and navigating these programs is essential to effectively accessing available support and services.

- Social Security Administration: https://www.ssa.gov
- Medicare: https://www.medicare.gov

- Medicaid: The official Medicaid website varies by state. You can find your state's Medicaid website by searching "[Your State] Medicaid" on a search engine.

Insurance Options

Long-term care insurance and life insurance with living benefits offer additional financial protection. Careful consideration and consultation with advisors ensure that chosen policies align with the caregiver's and the individual's needs and financial situation.

Insurance options play a crucial role in providing financial protection and peace of mind for individuals and their families, particularly in the context of long-term care and end-of-life planning.

- Long-Term Care Insurance: Long-term care insurance is designed to cover the costs associated with long-term care services, such as nursing home care, assisted living facilities, and in-home care. This type of insurance can help alleviate the financial burden of long-term care expenses, which can be significant and may not be fully covered by other forms of insurance or government programs like Medicare. Long-term care insurance policies vary in coverage options, benefit amounts, and eligibility criteria, so it's essential to carefully review and compare policies to find one that best suits your needs and budget.
- Life Insurance with Living Benefits: Life insurance policies with living benefits, also known as accelerated death benefits, offer additional financial protection by providing access to a portion of the death benefit while the insured is still alive, typically in the event of a

terminal illness or chronic condition requiring long-term care. These living benefits can help individuals cover medical expenses, long-term care costs, or other financial needs during their lifetime, providing valuable support and flexibility when it's needed most.

When considering insurance options for long-term care and end-of-life planning, it's essential to assess your needs, preferences, and financial situation carefully. Consulting with insurance professionals, financial advisors, and legal experts can help you navigate the complexities of insurance policies and make informed decisions that align with your goals and priorities. By exploring different insurance options and securing appropriate coverage, you can help ensure financial security and peace of mind for yourself and your loved ones in the face of long-term care needs and end-of-life expenses.

Beware of Scams

In the realm of financial planning and protection, the risk of scams and financial exploitation, particularly concerning dementia cases, poses a significant threat. Taking steps to prevent such abuse is essential, requiring vigilance and proactive measures. Helpful tips for safeguarding against these risks include:

- The monitoring of financial accounts for unusual activities.
- The establishment of trusted contact notifications with financial institutions.
- The education of the person with dementia on the common tactics employed by scammers.
- The safeguarding of Social Security numbers.

Choosing individuals entrusted with financial powers of attorney is crucial for guarding against scams and financial abuse. They must demonstrate integrity and trustworthiness to act in the best interest of the person in decline. By taking these precautions, caregivers shield their loved ones from exploitation and uphold the integrity of the meticulously crafted financial strategy designed to ensure their care and well-being.

In the realm of dementia care, where uncertainty prevails, and the landscape evolves with the disease's progression, financial planning, and protection serve as anchors of stability. They offer security and assure caregivers that they have utilized every resource and strategy available to construct a stronghold of support capable of weathering the challenges of the disease. This intricate and demanding undertaking is driven by a commitment to the welfare of the person with dementia, ensuring that each financial decision and protective measure is executed with care.

Safeguarding Your Social Security Number

Safeguarding your Social Security number (SSN) is crucial for protecting your identity and financial security. Here are some tips to help you keep your SSN safe:

- Memorize Your SSN: Avoid carrying your Social Security card with you unless necessary. Memorize your SSN instead of writing it down or carrying it in your wallet.
- Be Cautious with Sharing: Be cautious about who you share your SSN with. Only provide it when absolutely necessary, such as for employment, tax purposes, or government benefits.
- Secure Your Documents: Keep important documents containing your SSN, such as your Social Security card,

birth certificate, and tax forms, in a safe and secure location, preferably locked away.

- Monitor Your Credit Reports: Regularly monitor your credit reports from the three major credit bureaus (Equifax, Experian, and TransUnion) to detect any suspicious activity or unauthorized use of your SSN.
- Protect Your Personal Information Online: Be vigilant about protecting your personal information online. Avoid sharing your SSN or other sensitive information through email or on unsecured websites. Use strong, unique passwords for your online accounts and enable two-factor authentication whenever possible.
- Beware of Scams: Be wary of unsolicited calls, emails, or messages requesting your SSN or personal information. Scammers often pose as government agencies or financial institutions to trick individuals into divulging their SSNs. Never provide your SSN to unknown or unverified sources.
- Shred Documents: Before disposing of any documents containing your SSN or other sensitive information, shred them to prevent identity theft.
- Keep Your Devices Secure: Protect your electronic devices with passwords or biometric authentication and keep them updated with the latest security patches and antivirus software to prevent unauthorized access to your SSN stored on your devices.
- Report Lost or Stolen Documents: If your Social Security card or other documents containing your SSN are lost or stolen, report it to the Social Security Administration and consider placing a fraud alert or credit freeze on your credit reports.

Following these tips and staying vigilant can help safeguard your Social Security number and reduce the risk of identity theft and financial fraud.

ESSENTIAL LEGAL DOCUMENTS AND PLANNING

Combining legal and financial planning establishes a protective shield around the caregiver and the care recipient, shielding them from potential uncertainties that could disrupt their care and stability. This comprehensive planning, meticulous and thorough, encompasses various elements ranging from drafting wills and establishing trusts to appointing powers of attorney, ensuring that financial and care decisions align with the wishes and aspirations of both parties. Seeking guidance from legal professionals who are well-versed in estate planning and elder law is crucial, as they offer assurance and direction through the complexities of legal and financial matters. Rather than dwelling on future uncertainties, this proactive approach affirms individual autonomy, ensuring that personal values and preferences will be respected and safeguarded, regardless of what lies ahead.

Essential Documents

A checklist becomes invaluable, offering a clear view of the essential documents every caregiver should consider. These range from wills delineating the distribution of assets to living wills that articulate wishes regarding medical treatment. Guardianships, or legal conservatorships, empower a designated individual to make decisions on behalf of someone who can no longer do so themselves. Each document serves a specific purpose, acting as a safeguard, a declaration of intent and protection that spans financial, medical, and personal care considerations.

Several essential documents are recommended for end-of-life planning to ensure your wishes are respected and your affairs are handled appropriately. These documents include:

- Advance Directive: This document allows you to specify your preferences for medical care and appoint a healthcare proxy to make decisions on your behalf if you cannot. It typically includes a living will and a healthcare power of attorney.
- Living Will: A living will outline your preferences for medical treatment in specific situations, such as life support, resuscitation, and pain management.
- Healthcare Power of Attorney (Healthcare Proxy): This document appoints someone you trust to make healthcare decisions for you if you are incapacitated and unable to communicate your wishes.
- Do Not Resuscitate (DNR) Order: A DNR order instructs medical personnel not to perform CPR or other life-saving measures if your heart stops or if you stop breathing.
- Financial Power of Attorney: This document designates someone to manage your financial affairs if you become incapacitated.
- Will or Trust: A will or trust outlines how you want your assets to be distributed after your death and may appoint guardians for minor children.
- Beneficiary Designations: Ensure that beneficiary designations on insurance policies, retirement accounts, and other assets are up to date.
- Organ and Tissue Donation: If you wish to donate organs or tissues after your death, you can document your preferences in an organ and tissue donation form.

- Funeral or Burial Instructions: Provide instructions for your funeral or burial preferences, including any specific requests or arrangements you would like to be made. Share this information with your loved ones and consider pre-planning or pre-paying for funeral expenses if possible.
- Passwords and Account Information: Compile a list of important passwords and account information so your loved ones can access necessary accounts and digital assets.

These documents can vary depending on your personal circumstances and legal requirements in your jurisdiction. Reviewing and updating these documents regularly is important to ensure they accurately reflect your wishes. Consulting with an attorney specializing in estate planning can help you create a comprehensive plan tailored to your needs.

Remember that planning for the final stages of life is a deeply personal process, and there is no one-size-fits-all approach. Take the time to consider your values, beliefs, and virtues, and involve your loved ones in the process to ensure that your wishes are honored.

Protecting Assets and Rights

Strategies for safeguarding the assets and rights of those with dementia are diverse and should be tailored to their unique circumstances. They include setting up trusts to secure finances while preserving eligibility for public aid and establishing powers of attorney for decision-making support. These measures go beyond financial planning, embodying love and reverence and prioritizing the dignity and legacy of the person you care for.

Consider a scenario where someone in the early stages of dementia, guided by an elder law attorney, creates a trust. This proactive step, taken while they are still able to articulate their preferences, ensures that their assets support their care and family while preserving access to essential benefits. It is a thoughtful approach that combines financial wisdom with deep concern for the individual's well-being and independence.

In addressing the legal aspects of dementia care, families and caregivers lay the groundwork for future protection and foresight today. Honoring the individual's wishes ensures dignified care and respect for their estate. This intricate process is rooted in the fundamental act of nurturing someone's future, ensuring their security remains intact as circumstances evolve.

Selecting a Power of Attorney

Appointing a Power of Attorney (POA) is crucial to navigating the changing needs and decisions. This designated individual becomes a guiding light, leading through the uncertainties of financial and healthcare decisions with the authority to act in the best interests of the person with dementia. The role of a Power of Attorney embodies the profound trust placed by one individual in another to make pivotal decisions regarding finances and health. This entrusted individual steps into the shoes of their authority and ensures continuity and stability in the care and management of affairs, often in moments fraught with vulnerability.

Understanding the responsibilities of the Power of Attorney is pivotal. These responsibilities encompass the management of finances and extend to making healthcare decisions that align with the vulnerable individual. The legal process begins with drafting the Power of Attorney document, which often requires notarization. The involvement of legal professionals specializing in elder law can ensure that this document meets the legal standards and solidifies its legitimacy.

Selecting the right person to serve as Power of Attorney necessitates a discerning eye, trustworthiness, and availability. It demands a deep dive into the dynamics of relationships and an assessment of the POA's capacity

There are several types of power of attorney (POA), each serving different purposes and granting varying degrees of authority to the appointed agent. Here are the main types:

- General Power of Attorney: This type of POA grants broad authority to the agent to act on behalf of the principal in various legal and financial matters. It is typically used for temporary situations or when the principal is unable to handle their affairs due to travel, illness, or other reasons.
- Limited or Specific Power of Attorney: A limited or specific POA grants the agent authority to perform only specific tasks or act on behalf of the principal in limited circumstances. For example, the POA may be limited to handling a particular financial transaction or signing specific documents.
- Durable Power of Attorney: A durable POA remains valid even if the principal becomes incapacitated or mentally incompetent. It allows the agent to continue managing the principal's affairs in such situations. This type of POA is often used for long-term planning and healthcare decision-making.
- Springing Power of Attorney: A springing POA becomes effective only under specific conditions specified by the principal, such as the principal becoming incapacitated.

It "springs" into effect when the specified condition occurs.

- Healthcare Power of Attorney (Healthcare Proxy): This type of POA specifically grants authority to the agent to make healthcare decisions on behalf of the principal if they are unable to do so. It is often used in conjunction with an advance directive or living will to ensure that the principal's medical wishes are followed.
- Financial Power of Attorney: A financial POA grants the agent authority to manage the principal's financial affairs, such as paying bills, managing investments, and accessing bank accounts. It can be general or limited in scope.
- Special Power of Attorney: A special POA grants the agent authority to perform specific tasks or transactions on behalf of the principal, such as buying or selling property, handling legal matters, or signing contracts.

When choosing the type of power of attorney, it's important to carefully consider the principal's specific needs and circumstances and consult legal professionals to ensure that the POA meets all legal requirements and adequately protects the principal's interests.

CHAPTER 8

EMBRACING CONNECTIONS

Whether as caregivers, family members, or friends, the way we connect and interact with individuals living with dementia can profoundly impact their well-being and quality of life. This chapter explores the importance of meaningful engagement in dementia care, offering insights and strategies to foster connection, dignity, and joy amidst the complexities of memory loss.

ENGAGING WITH OTHERS

This is important for individuals with dementia as it promotes social interaction, stimulates cognitive function, and enhances emotional wellness. Here are some ways individuals with dementia can engage with others:

- Join Social Groups: Encourage participation in social functions specifically designed for individuals with impaired memory, such as support groups, memory cafes, or day programs. These settings provide opportunities to connect with peers, share experiences, and engage in meaningful activities.

- Attend Community Events: Take part in public gatherings, such as local fairs, concerts, or art exhibitions, where individuals with dementia can interact with others in a more relaxed environment.
- Volunteer: Engage in volunteer activities tailored to their interests and abilities. Volunteering at local organizations, schools, or community centers allows individuals with dementia to contribute to their community while interacting.
- Interact with Pets: Spending time with pets can be therapeutic for individuals with dementia. Whether it is petting a cat or walking a dog, interacting with animals can provide comfort, companionship, and opportunities for engagement.
- Participate in Hobbies: Encourage children to engage in hobbies and activities they enjoy, such as gardening, painting, knitting, or playing musical instruments. Engaging in familiar activities can boost confidence, stimulate cognitive function, and develop connections with others with similar interests.
- Reminisce and Share Stories: Encourage reminiscence by looking through old photo albums, listening to music from their youth, or sharing stories about past experiences. Reminiscing can spark conversations, evoke positive memories, and strengthen social bonds with family and friends.
- Attend Social Gatherings: Attend family events, celebrations, or outings with friends to maintain social connections and relationships. Create opportunities for

individuals with dementia to interact with others in a supportive and familiar setting.

- Participate in Exercise Classes: Join exercise classes specifically designed for individuals with dementia, such as chair yoga, tai chi, or gentle stretching exercises. Physical activity not only promotes physical health but also provides opportunities for social interaction and engagement.
- Use Technology: Utilize technology to facilitate social connections, such as video calls with family members or online social networks for individuals with dementia. Virtual interactions can help individuals stay connected with loved ones and engage in conversations from the comfort of their homes.
- Encourage Group Activities: Participate in group activities such as board games, puzzles, or group exercise classes. Group activities create a sense of camaraderie, teamwork, and shared experiences, promoting social engagement and enjoyment.

By incorporating these strategies, individuals with dementia can actively engage with others, maintain social connections, and experience a sense of belonging and fulfillment in their community. Moments of feeling "normal" can boost morale and promote and prolong well-being.

REGULAR CHECK-INS AND TEAM COORDINATION

In the realm of dementia care, the strength of a support network lies in its ability to unite individual efforts into a collective force, benefiting both caregivers and those under their care. This segment delves into establishing and maintaining a care team—a coalition comprising family, friends, healthcare professionals, and community resources—dedicated to delivering comprehensive and empathetic care.

Regular check-ins and updates form the backbone of seamless teamwork within the care team. This ongoing exchange sustains the vitality of caregiving by ensuring that everyone remains informed and prepared to act as needed. Whether through a weekly email update or a shared calendar documenting appointments and shifts, these periodic updates serve as vital touchpoints for assessing the current state of the care plan and implementing any necessary adjustments. Such continual communication ensures that each member of the team remains attuned to the evolving needs of the care recipient, fostering a culture of coordination and collaboration among caregivers and facilitating effective, responsive care.

Digital Communication Platforms

In today's digital age, many tools and platforms facilitate seamless communication amongst care team members, ensuring everyone stays informed and engaged. Digital platforms like shared Google Docs for care logs, Slack channels for quick updates, or dedicated WhatsApp groups for daily check-ins offer accessible, immediate ways to share information, ask for help, or coordinate care tasks. This digital net catches the details large and small, ensuring no aspect of care falls through the cracks.

LEVERAGING COMMUNITY RESOURCES

Caring for someone with dementia can be challenging, but many local resources are available to help. By connecting with community services, caregivers can find support and assistance that ease the burden of caregiving.

Exploring Community Support for Dementia Care

- Learning about local services from healthcare professionals and online forums.
- Exploring directories, senior centers, and libraries for information.
- Accessing government assistance programs for additional support.
- Participating in support groups and workshops for caregivers and individuals with dementia.
- Building relationships with service providers to tailor care to individual needs.

Websites for Community Resources for Dementia Caregivers

- Alzheimer's Association Community Forums: The Alzheimer's Association hosts online forums where caregivers can connect with others facing similar challenges. Their website provides information on local chapters, support groups, educational programs, and community resources. Visit: Alzheimer's Association Community Forums.
- AgingCare.com Caregiver Forum: AgingCare.com offers a caregiver forum where individuals caring for older adults, including those with dementia, can ask questions, share experiences, and offer support to one another. Visit: AgingCare.com Caregiver Forum.
- Eldercare Locator: The Eldercare Locator is a public service provided by the U.S. Administration on Aging that

connects older adults and their caregivers with local support services and resources. Their website and toll-free hotline can help individuals locate services such as transportation, meal delivery, and adult day care centers in their community. Visit Eldercare Locator.com.

- MyAlzTeam: MyAlzTeam is a social network and support group for caregivers of people with Alzheimer's and dementia. Members can connect with others, ask questions, and share advice in a supportive online community. Visit: MyAlzTeam.com.
- Caring.com Caregiver Forum: Caring.com hosts a caregiver forum where individuals caring for loved ones with dementia can find support, guidance, and resources from fellow caregivers. Visit: Caring.com Caregiver Forum.
- DailyStrength - Alzheimer's/Dementia Support Group: DailyStrength is an online support community with a dedicated group for Alzheimer's and dementia caregivers. Members can connect with others, share stories, and offer encouragement. Visit DailyStrength - Alzheimer's/Dementia Support Group.com.
- National Institute on Aging (NIA): The NIA provides information and resources on aging-related topics, including dementia care and support services. Its website offers articles, guides, and links to additional resources to help individuals find local services and support. Visit the National Institute on Aging.
- Local Government Websites: Many local government websites have sections dedicated to senior services and support programs. These websites may provide information on local resources for dementia care, such as senior centers, adult daycare programs, and caregiver

support groups. Searching for "[Your City/County] senior services" or "[Your State] department of aging" can help you find relevant information.

These online communities and forums provide valuable opportunities for dementia caregivers to connect with others, seek advice, and find support in their caregiving journey.

USING TECHNOLOGY TO CONNECT AND MANAGE CARE

In an era where digital innovation reshapes landscapes across every facet of human endeavor, dementia care, too, finds itself under the transformative gaze of technology. This section unfolds the narrative of digital tools and platforms not merely as instruments of convenience but as vital parts in the machinery of care coordination, offering caregivers a life jacket in the rough seas of their responsibilities.

Digital Tools and Platforms for Care Coordination

Several digital tools and platforms are available to facilitate dementia care coordination and communication among caregivers, family members, and healthcare professionals. Here are some examples:

- CareZone: CareZone is a mobile app that helps caregivers organize and manage important information, such as medication lists, appointments, and notes. It also allows for secure sharing of information with family members and healthcare providers.
- CaringBridge: CaringBridge is a website and mobile app that allows caregivers to create a private online journal to

update family and friends about the care recipient's health and progress. It provides a centralized platform for communication and support.

- Lotsa Helping Hands: Lotsa Helping Hands is an online caregiving coordination platform that allows caregivers to create a private community where family and friends can sign up to help with tasks such as meal delivery, transportation, and respite care.
- Caregiver Action Network (CAN) Toolbox: CAN offers a toolbox with resources and tools for caregivers, including checklists, worksheets, and guides to help with care coordination and planning.
- AARP Caregiving App: AARP offers a caregiving app that provides resources, tips, and tools for caregivers, including a medication tracker, appointment calendar, and journal for recording notes and observations.
- Caregiver Support App by Alzheimer's Association: The Alzheimer's Association offers a caregiver support app that provides information, resources, and tools specifically for dementia caregivers, including tips for managing behaviors and accessing support services.
- HomeHero: HomeHero is a platform that connects caregivers with families seeking in-home care services. It provides tools for scheduling, communication, and tracking care tasks and activities.
- LifePod: LifePod is a voice-activated virtual caregiver assistant designed to provide reminders, medication alerts, and companionship for individuals with dementia. Caregivers can also use the platform to monitor and manage care remotely.
- CareMerge: CareMerge is a care coordination platform designed for senior living communities and long-term

care facilities. It enables staff members to coordinate care plans, communicate with families, and track residents' health and well-being in real-time.

- MemoryWell: MemoryWell is a digital storytelling platform that allows caregivers to create personalized life stories for individuals with dementia. These stories can be shared with healthcare providers to provide insight into the care recipient's preferences, interests, and life history.

These digital tools and platforms can help streamline care coordination, improve communication among caregivers and healthcare providers, and provide support and resources to caregivers throughout their caregiving journey.

Embracing Telehealth for Dementia Care

The integration of telehealth services into the world of dementia care marks a significant evolution, one that brings the expertise of healthcare professionals into the comfort of the home. This digital bridge between caregiver and clinician can dismantle barriers to care, offering options where consultations, therapy sessions, and support services are accessible without needing physical travel. For individuals with dementia and their caregivers, this means alleviating the logistical and emotional strain associated with visits to clinics and preserving energy for care tasks that demand their attention at home. The efficacy of telehealth lies in its convenience and capacity to maintain continuity of care, ensuring that medical oversight remains constant, regardless of the circumstances that might otherwise hinder access to services. Note that some healthcare plans have their own platform; check with your doctor for this option.

For example:

- Virtual Doctor Visits: Platforms like Teladoc and Amwell enable individuals with dementia and their caregivers to consult with healthcare providers remotely, reducing the need for physical travel to clinics.
- Online Therapy Sessions: Services such as Talkspace and BetterHelp offer online therapy sessions for individuals with dementia and their caregivers. These sessions provide emotional support and guidance from licensed therapists.
- Remote Monitoring Devices: Devices like GrandCare Systems and CarePredict use remote monitoring technology to track vital signs and activity levels, allowing healthcare providers to assess the health and well-being of individuals with dementia from a distance.

By leveraging telehealth services, individuals with dementia and their caregivers can minimize the logistical and emotional burdens associated with in-person visits to healthcare facilities. This convenience fosters continuity of care, ensuring that medical oversight remains consistent regardless of the circumstances.

Technology Training for Caregivers

Technology can greatly improve dementia care, but caregivers must know how to use digital tools effectively. Providing technology training is crucial. This training, offered through workshops, online tutorials, and support hotlines, helps caregivers understand and use apps, platforms, and devices. It empowers them to create modern and effective care plans. Technology is seen as essential, not just an extra, in providing quality care.

In dementia care, technology is a helpful tool that connects caregivers and improves their skills. It includes tools for coordinating care, online communities, telehealth services, and training. While it may seem complicated, the goal is to help caregivers provide compassionate care and stay connected, even during difficult times.

- Local Senior Centers: Many senior centers offer technology classes and workshops specifically designed for older adults and caregivers. These classes cover topics such as basic computer skills, internet navigation, and using smartphones and tablets.
- Libraries: Public libraries often offer free technology training programs and resources for individuals of all ages. Caregivers can inquire about computer classes, one-on-one tutoring sessions, and access to online learning platforms.
- Online Learning Platforms: Websites like LinkedIn Learning, Udemy, and Coursera offer a wide range of online courses and tutorials on technology topics. Caregivers can explore courses on basic computer skills, smartphone usage, social media, and more at their own pace.
- Tech-Savvy Friends and Family: Caregivers can reach out to friends and family members who are comfortable with technology for informal training sessions and assistance. This personalized approach can be tailored to the caregiver's specific needs and learning style.
- Caregiver Support Groups: Some caregiver support groups and organizations offer technology training as part of their services. These sessions may cover topics such as

using telehealth platforms, managing healthcare apps, and accessing online resources for caregiving support.

- AARP TEK Workshops: AARP offers free TEK (Technology Education & Knowledge) workshops that provide hands-on training and support for older adults and caregivers. Workshops cover topics such as using smartphones, tablets, and other devices to stay connected and informed.
- Local Community Colleges: Community colleges often offer continuing education courses on technology topics for learners of all ages. Caregivers can explore courses on computer basics, internet safety, and digital communication skills.

By utilizing these resources, caregivers can enhance their technology skills and feel more confident in using digital tools and devices to support their caregiving responsibilities.

COLLABORATING WITH NEIGHBORS AND LOCAL SERVICES

The community can offer support beyond the confines of immediate family and specialized care teams. Neighbors and local services possess the capacity to bring mutual understanding and shared responsibility, holding the potential to transform neighborhoods into sanctuaries of support for those navigating the challenges of dementia.

Building a Local Support Network

It begins with the act of reaching out and connecting with those around them. This outreach, though it may start as a ripple—a conversation over a fence, an introduction at a local meeting—can grow into a strong community network. Tips for building these relationships include being open and sharing information about dementia to help others understand. This openness can lead to empathy and practical support, from arranging shared meals to offering companionship. Each small action contributes to a caring community.

Local services that can provide assistance to individuals dealing with dementia and their caregivers include:

- Senior Centers: Senior centers often offer programs and activities tailored to individuals with dementia, such as memory cafes, support groups, and educational workshops.
- Adult Day Care Centers: Adult day care centers provide supervised activities and socialization opportunities for older adults, including those with dementia, allowing caregivers to take a break from caregiving responsibilities.
- Community Health Clinics: Community health clinics may offer dementia screenings, medical consultations, and referrals to specialized services for diagnosis and treatment.
- Home Health Agencies: Home health agencies can provide skilled nursing care, personal care assistance, and respite services for caregivers.
- Transportation Services: Transportation services can help individuals with dementia attend medical appointments, social outings, and other activities, reducing isolation and promoting engagement in the community.
- Meals on Wheels: Meals on Wheels programs deliver nutritious meals to homebound seniors, including those with dementia, ensuring they have access to healthy food

and alleviating the burden of meal preparation for caregivers.

- Legal and Financial Services: Legal and financial services can assist caregivers with estate planning, guardianship arrangements, and accessing benefits and resources to support their caregiving responsibilities.
- Faith-based Organizations: Churches, synagogues, mosques, and other religious institutions often provide support and assistance to individuals and families affected by dementia, including pastoral care, support groups, and volunteer services.
- Community Organizations: Nonprofit organizations and community groups dedicated to aging, caregiving, and dementia may offer a wide range of services and resources, such as educational programs, respite care, and caregiver support services.
- Social Services Agencies: Social services agencies can connect individuals and families affected by dementia with community resources and support services, such as case management, counseling, and advocacy assistance.

Living in Rural Areas

Living in a rural area with limited resources can pose challenges for individuals dealing with dementia and their caregivers. However, there are still steps they can take to seek support and assistance.

- Online Resources: Utilize online resources such as support groups, educational websites, and forums dedicated to dementia care. These platforms can provide valuable information, advice, and emotional support, even if local services are limited.

- Telehealth Services: Explore telehealth options for remotely accessing medical consultations, therapy sessions, and support services. Many healthcare providers offer telehealth appointments, allowing individuals to receive care without needing to travel long distances.
- Community Outreach: Take the initiative to connect with neighbors, community organizations, and local leaders to raise awareness about the needs of individuals with dementia and caregivers in rural areas. This can potentially lead to the development of new support services and resources.
- Faith-based Organizations: Reach out to churches, synagogues, mosques, and other religious institutions in the community. They may offer pastoral care, support groups, and volunteer services that can provide emotional and practical assistance.
- Volunteer Networks: Explore volunteer networks and service organizations in the area. Volunteers may be willing to provide transportation, respite care, or companionship to individuals with dementia and their caregivers.
- Local Libraries: Visit the local library to access books, DVDs, and other resources on dementia care. Librarians may also be able to provide information on community services and support groups.
- Regional Agencies: Contact regional or state-level agencies and organizations dedicated to aging, caregiving, and dementia. They may offer information, referrals, and assistance in accessing services and resources available in rural areas.

- Creative Solutions: Consider creative solutions to meet specific needs. For example, forming a caregiver support group or social club with other individuals in the community facing similar challenges can provide mutual support and companionship.

While living in a rural area may present unique obstacles, seeking out available resources and building connections within the community can help individuals dealing with dementia and their caregivers find support and assistance.

Collaborative Safety Plans

The reality and probability of wandering, a common and distressing manifestation of dementia, necessitates a community-wide approach to safety—a collaborative effort that transforms individual concern into collective action. Crafting safety plans with neighbors involves sharing information and equipping those in our vicinity with the knowledge needed to recognize and gently guide a lost individual back to the safety of their homes. This collective vigilance is further reinforced by establishing visible identifiers—a bracelet, a garment, or even a door sign—that signal to the informed observer the need for gentle intervention. Such plans can be co-created with the input of local law enforcement and dementia support organizations. Implementing the proverb that "it takes a village" turns the concept of community watch into a tangible pillar of safety for those at risk of wandering.

Community Awareness

As this chapter closes we pause to consider the significant role of community in the caregiving journey. We harness the power of neighbors and local services by reaching out, sharing, and working together. This communal effort not only enhances the lives of those in need but also fosters a culture of empathy, understanding, and support that extends beyond caregiving. As we look ahead, let us carry the lessons of collaboration with us, guiding us through the challenges of dementia in the light of community cooperation. We reflect on the profound impact of community on the journey of care. Utilizing neighbors and local services is grounded in the simple act of reaching out, sharing, and engaging in a shared endeavor. This communal approach not only enriches the lives of people in decline but also creates a broader culture of empathy, understanding, and support—a legacy that transcends the immediate challenges of caregiving and touches the heart of the community itself. As we move forward, let us carry the lessons of collaboration, holding them as flares that light our way through the complexities of dementia.

Embracing the Grief

The loss of a loved one who battled dementia can be uniquely challenging due to the prolonged nature of the illness and the gradual decline in cognitive function. Coping with grief in such circumstances may involve several strategies:

- Acknowledging Your Feelings: It's crucial to recognize and accept the range of emotions you may experience, including sadness, anger, guilt, relief, or even numbness. Each person's grieving process is unique, and there's no right or wrong way to feel.
- Seeking Support: Lean on family members, friends, or support groups who understand the complexities of grieving a loved one with dementia. Sharing your feelings and memories can be therapeutic, and connecting with others who have gone through similar experiences can provide comfort and validation.

- Reflecting on the Relationship: Take time to honor and reflect on the relationship you had with the individual who passed away. Celebrate their life by reminiscing about meaningful moments, cherished memories, and the impact they had on your life and others.
- Self-Care: Engage in self-care activities that promote physical, emotional, and mental well-being. This could include exercise, mindfulness or relaxation techniques, journaling, spending time in nature, or engaging in hobbies and interests that bring you joy.
- Seeking Professional Help: If you're struggling to cope with grief or experiencing prolonged distress, consider seeking support from a therapist, counselor, or grief specialist. Professional guidance can provide you with coping strategies, validation, and a safe space to explore your feelings.
- Honoring Their Legacy: Find meaningful ways to honor the memory of your loved one with dementia. This could involve creating a memory book or collage, participating in fundraising or awareness events for dementia research or support organizations, or planting a tree or garden in their honor.
- Allowing Yourself Time: Grieving is a process that takes time, and there's no set timeline for healing. Be patient and compassionate with yourself as you navigate the ups and downs of grief. Allow yourself to feel whatever emotions arise and understand that healing happens gradually.

Remember that grief is a natural response to loss, and it's okay to seek help and support as you navigate this challenging journey.

Thank you for joining me on this compassionate journey through the pages of 'Dementia Caregiver's Guide.' As we reach the end of this book, may you carry with you the invaluable insights, practical advice, and heartfelt encouragement found within these chapters. May these words serve as a guiding light in your caregiving journey, offering comfort, strength, and support during both the challenging moments and the moments of grace. Remember, you are not alone on this path. Together, we can navigate the complexities of dementia caregiving with compassion, resilience, and unwavering love. Wishing you peace, patience, and profound moments of connection as you continue to care for your loved one with dementia.

Simply scan the QR code below to leave your review:

CONCLUSION

As we near the end of our journey together, let's take a moment to look back on the path we've walked. Dementia caregiving is a challenging journey filled with ups and downs, where moments of deep connection mix with tough challenges. You've faced each day with courage and a strong commitment to those you care for. This journey requires practical skills, empathy, and resilience.

Our goal has been to understand dementia better, to see beyond its surface, and to understand how it affects individuals and families. This understanding is crucial for providing compassionate and effective care. It helps us support our loved ones and honor their humanity throughout their journey with dementia.

Together, we've explored important strategies for effective caregiving. Each chapter has provided tools to improve your caregiving, from better communication and behavior management to personal care and safety practices. We've discussed legal and financial planning and the value of building a supportive community with healthcare professionals, neighbors, and fellow caregivers online.

Now, it's time to take action. Use the strategies that resonate with you, seek support when needed, and work to raise awareness of dementia in your community. Remember, you're not alone in this journey. There's a vast network of caregivers, professionals, and advocates who share your commitment and can offer help and advice.

Amidst the difficulties, there's always hope. Knowing you have the tools, resources, and inner strength to care effectively is empowering. Every day, you make a difference in the lives of those you care for, showing the power of love and resilience.

Thank you for walking this path with me. May you move forward with confidence and compassion, embracing each day of your caregiving journey with strength and grace.

REFERENCES

Coetzer, K. Nov. 2017. "There will come a time when your loved one will be gone, and you will find comfort in the fact that you were their caregiver."

10 Early Signs and Symptoms of Alzheimer's & Dementia https://www.alz.org/alzheimers-dementia/10_signs

Understanding Different Types of Dementia https://www.nia.nih.gov/health/alzheimers-and-dementia/understanding-different-types-dementia

Dementia - communication - Better Health Channel https://www.betterhealth.vic.gov.au/health/conditionsandtreatments/dementia-communication

Family caregivers of people with dementia - PMC https://www.ncbi.nlm.nih.gov/pmc/articles/PMC3181916/

Communication and Alzheimer's https://www.alz.org/help-support/caregiving/daily-care/communications

Non-verbal communication and dementia https://www.alzheimers.org.uk/about-dementia/symptoms-and-diagnosis/symptoms/non-verbal-communication-and-dementia

Use of the physical environment to support everyday ... https://www.ncbi.nlm.nih.gov/pmc/articles/PMC6039869/

For Caregivers of People with Alzheimer's or Other Forms of ... https://theconversation-project.org/wp-content/uploads/2020/12/DementiaGuide.pdf

Recognition and Management of Behavioral Disturbances ... https://www.ncbi.nlm.nih.gov/pmc/articles/PMC181170/

What equipment can improve the home of a person with ... https://www.alzheimers.org.uk/get-support/staying-independent/what-equipment-improve-adapt-home-person-dementia

Alzheimer's and Dementia Support Groups https://alzfdn.org/caregiving-resources/alzheimers-and-dementia-support-groups/

Bathing, Dressing, and Grooming: Alzheimer's Caregiving Tips https://www.nia.nih.gov/health/alzheimers-caregiving/bathing-dressing-and-grooming-alzheimers-caregiving-tips

ESPEN guidelines on nutrition in dementia https://www.clinicalnutritionjournal.com/article/S0261-5614(15)00237-X/fulltext

Adaptive Clothing for People Living with Dementia https://www.theablelabel.com/en-us/collections/alzheimers-society-adaptive-clothing

Medicines management issues in dementia and coping strategies https://www.ncbi.nlm.nih.gov/pmc/articles/PMC6282522/

Financial and Legal Planning for Caregivers https://www.alz.org/help-support/caregiving/financial-legal-planning

The Latest Advances in the Diagnosis and Treatment ... - Cureus https://www.cureus.com/articles/210259-the-latest-advances-in-the-diagnosis-and-treatment-of-dementia

Caregiver stress: Tips for taking care of yourself - Mayo Clinic https://www.mayoclinic.org/healthy-lifestyle/stress-management/in-depth/caregiver-stress/art-20044784

Federal Funding and Support Opportunities for Respite https://archrespite.org/library/federal-funding-and-support-opportunities-for-respite/?utm_source=rss&utm_medium=rss&utm_campaign=federal-funding-and-support-opportunities-for-respite

Dementia care navigation: Building toward a common ... https://www.ncbi.nlm.nih.gov/pmc/articles/PMC10392594/

22 Top Caregiver Support Groups: Online and In-Person https://www.aplaceformom.com/caregiver-resources/articles/caregiver-support-groups

Legal Documents https://www.alz.org/help-support/caregiving/financial-legal-planning/legal-documents

Long-Term Care - Alzheimer's Association https://www.alz.org/help-support/caregiving/care-options/long-term-care

A Guide to Creating a Dementia-Friendly Home https://alzfdn.org/wp-content/uploads/2021/03/The-Apartment-Guide-web.pdf

Collaborative transdisciplinary team approach for dementia care https://www.ncbi.nlm.nih.gov/pmc/articles/PMC4308691/

Studies Show Benefits of Caregiver Support Programs https://www.nih.gov/news-events/nih-research-matters/studies-show-benefits-caregiver-support-programs

Use of technology and social media in dementia care https://www.ncbi.nlm.nih.gov/pmc/articles/PMC8040150/

Legal and Financial Planning for People Living With Dementia https://order.nia.nih.gov/publication/legal-and-financial-planning-for-people-living-with-dementia

National Family Caregiver Support Program: https://acl.gov/programs/support-caregivers/national-family-caregiver-support-program

National Institute on Aging. (2022). Alzheimer's Disease Fact Sheet. Retrieved from https://www.nia.nih.gov/health/alzheimers-disease-fact-sheet.

Made in the USA
Columbia, SC
15 November 2024

46586692R00093